What Are They Saying About Acts?

Mark Allan Powell

PAULIST PRESS
New York/Mahwah, N.J.

Library of Congress Cataloging-in-Publication Data

Powell, Mark Allan, 1953–
    What are they saying about Acts? / Mark Allan Powell.
      p.   cm.
    Includes bibliographical references.
    ISBN 0-8091-3279-6 (pbk.)
    1. Bible. N.T. Acts—Criticism, interpretation, etc.—
History—20th century. 2. Bible. N.T. Acts—Criticism,
interpretation, etc. I. Title.
BS2625.2.P694   1991
226.6'06'0904—dc20

                  91-27685
                  CIP

Published by Paulist Press
997 Macarthur Boulevard
Mahwah, New Jersey 07430

Printed and bound in the
United States of America

Contents

In memory of my father
Robert Delafield Powell
(1919–1989)

Abbreviations

AB	Anchor Bible
ACNT	Augsburg Commentary on the New Testament
AnBib	Analecta Biblica
ATANT	Abhandlungen zur Theologie des Alten und Neuen Testaments
ANQ	*Andover Newton Quarterly*
ASNU	Acta seminarii neotestamentici upsaliensis
BbB	Bonner biblische Beiträge
BETL	Biblioteca ephemiridum theologicarum lovaniensium
BR	*Biblical Research*
BTB	*Biblical Theology Bulletin*
BU	Biblische Untersuchungen
BWANT	Beiträge zur Wissenschaft vom Alten und Neuen Testament
BZ	*Biblische Zeitschrift*

CB	*Cultura biblica*
CBQ	*Catholic Biblical Quarterly*
CTM	*Concordia Theological Monthly*
Cur TM	*Currents in Theology and Mission*
Egl Theol	*Église et Théologie*
Ehpr	Études d'histoire et de philosophie religieuses
EvQ	*The Evangelical Quarterly*
ExpT	*Expository Times*
FB	Facet Books
FGnKaL	Forschungen zur Geschichte des neutestamentlichen Kanons und der altkirchlichen Literatur
FRLANT	Forschungen zur Religion und Literatur des Alten und Neuen Testaments
FzB	Forschung zur Bibel
GNS	Good News Studies
Herm	Hermeneia
HTS	Harvard Theological Studies
IC	Interpretation Commentaries
Int	*Interpretation*
JBL	*Journal of Biblical Literature*

JR	*Journal of Religion*
JRS	*Journal of Roman Studies*
JSNT	*Journal for the Study of the New Testament*
JSNTSS	Journal for the Study of the New Testament Supplement Series
JTS	*Journal of Theological Studies*
LD	Lectio Divina
LEC	Library of Early Christianity
NICNT	New International Commentary on the New Testament
NovT	*Novum Testamentum*
NovTSup	Novum Testamentum Supplements
NTAbh	Neotestamentliche Abhandlungen
NTS	New Testament Studies
NTS	*New Testament Studies*
NTSMS	New Testament Studies Monograph Series
OBT	Overtures to Biblical Theology
OIC	*One in Christ*
PC	Proclamation Commentaries
PT	*Poetics Today*

RB	*Revue biblique*
RevistB	*Revista biblica*
RevExp	*Review and Expositor*
RevistB	*Revista biblica*
RevScRel	*Revue des sciences religieuses*
RHPR	*Revue d'histoire et de philosophie religieuses*
RSR	*Recherches de science religieuse*
RevScRel	*Revue des sciences religieuses*
SANT	Studien zum Alten und Neuen Testament
SB	Stuttgarter Bibelstudien
SBLMS	Society of Biblical Literature Monograph Series
SBLDS	Society of Biblical Literature Dissertation Series
SBT	Studies in Biblical Theology
SN	Studia Neotestamentica
SNTSMS	Society for New Testament Studies Monograph Series
SNTSU	Studien zum Neuen Testament und seiner Umwelt
SNTW	Studies of the New Testament and Its World
SUNT	Studien zur Umwelt des Neuen Testaments
SZNT	Studien zum Neuen Testament

TDNT	*Theological Dictionary of the New Testament*
ThStK	*Theologische Studien und Kritiken*
TNTC	Tyndale New Testament Commentaries
US	*Una Sancta*
WMANT	Wissenschaftliche Monographien zum Alten und Neuen Testament
WS	Walderberger Studien
ZNW	*Zeitschrift für die neutestamentliche Wissenschaft*

Introduction

In some ways, the book of Acts has never been a "bestseller."[1] It was not accepted into the Christian canon as enthusiastically as were the gospels and it was not as widely read in antiquity. In the fourth century, John Chrysostom complained that some people did not even know of the book's existence.[2] The problem was that Acts was not customarily used in Christian preaching. In our own day, it is read in the lectionary only during the Easter season and on the day of Pentecost.

The book, however, has gained a grass-roots following among the general public of Christianity. Its stories fascinate, amuse, challenge, and edify readers of all persuasions. Some of its special features—an emphasis on evangelism, a lively interest in spiritual experiences, a marked concern for the poor—have made it the most widely read book in some people's Bibles.

Acts has not met with disinterest in academic circles either. Bible scholars have produced a wealth of studies on Acts in recent years, interpreting the book from several different perspectives. Along with the gospel of Luke, Acts has been called a "storm-center in contemporary scholarship."[3]

This book provides an overview of current scholarship on Acts. Selected works are surveyed, with no pretense at being exhaustive. Rather, the focus is on identification of trends and delineation of representative positions.

Chapter 1 treats three matters that often determine how Acts is to be interpreted: the relationship it bears to Luke's gospel, the literary genre to which it should be assigned, and the purpose for which it was written. Chapter 2 deals with basic questions regarding the composition of the work—who wrote it, what sources were used, how it was organized, and so on.

The remaining chapters focus on three different perspectives from which Acts is sometimes interpreted. Chapters 3 and 4 present results of the major approach today—redaction criticism—by outlining scholarly opinions on the theology of Acts. Several issues are presented: theology proper, christology, the role of the Spirit, eschatology, and ecclesiology. Chapter 5 takes a different tack and discusses ways in which Acts is used and evaluated as a historical record. Chapter 6 treats a relatively new development in biblical studies: the use of modern literary-critical methods to describe the effect of Acts on its readers.

This book is intended for laity, students, and pastors. As such, it may fulfill a variety of functions. It will, I hope, provide a non-technical survey for those who would like to know a little something about this subject but have no intention of pursuing the matter further. For others, I hope it will serve as a suitable introduction to the field, one that offers a general overview as well as some guidance on where to go next. Still others may find help in updating and synthesizing knowledge obtained previously. Or, if used sporadically rather than read straight through, the book may serve as something of a map, that is, as an aid in locating particular ideas on the terrain of broad opinion.

This book, like the book of Acts itself, is a sequel. I have tried to avoid repetition of matters discussed in my earlier volume, *What Are They Saying About Luke?*,[4] but that has not always been possible. Many topics of significance for Luke's gospel are also important for the study of Acts. I have not omitted any matter essential to an understanding of Acts simply because it was treated in my first book, but I have tended to focus most heavily on matters endemic to Luke's second volume. Specific studies referred to briefly here are sometimes discussed in more detail in my book on the gospel.

I express my appreciation, once again, to Lawrence Boadt and to Paulist Press for granting me the opportunity to present this study, and to Trinity Lutheran Seminary in Columbus, Ohio, for its continuing commitment to encourage and support biblical scholarship in service to the church. My wife, Charlotte, and my children,

David and Michael, provide me with a context of emotional well-being and support in which projects such as this and, indeed, life itself can be undertaken with joy.

Finally, I am grateful once again to Melissa C. Curtis, secretary to the faculty at Trinity Lutheran Seminary, for her work of typing and correcting the manuscript. My readers all benefit from her commitment and expertise, even if they are unable to experience in person the grace, charm, wit, and enthusiasm enjoyed by all who know her.

1
Luke's Second Volume

There is nothing else in the New Testament quite like the book of Acts. In our Bibles, it lies between the gospels and the letters, a unique entry in the canon of scripture.

Of the four gospel writers, only Luke thought it necessary to produce a sequel, to continue the story of what Jesus "began to do and teach" (Acts 1:1) with a narrative of the early church. Scholars have proposed a number of reasons to explain why Luke did this, and some of these will be discussed in this chapter. First, however, we will deal with two other matters: the relationship that the second volume bears to the first, and the genre of literature to which it should be ascribed.

Relationship to the Gospel

Before 1927, New Testament scholars talked about "Luke" and "Acts" as though they were two different books that probably came from the same person. Since that date, they have become increasingly accustomed to speaking of "Luke-Acts" as a single book that exists in two volumes.

What happened in 1927? Henry Cadbury published the first edition of what was to be one of the most influential New Testament studies of the twentieth century.[1] Called *The Making of Luke-Acts*, the book investigated factors in the composition of both works, with special attention to their literary style and unity. In retrospect, the title of Cadbury's book contained an unintentional pun, for it was his book itself that made "Luke-Acts" an identifiable entity in its own right.

To the average Bible reader, this may seem strange. Luke and Acts are two different books, separated in our Bibles by the gospel of John. But today many Bible scholars regard this as a fluke of manuscript arrangement. F. F. Bruce thinks that what Luke actually wrote was one book on the history of Christian origins.[2] The book had to be produced in two volumes because it was too long to fit on a single scroll. Still, Luke intended for the two volumes to be read together. Unfortunately, when Luke's writings were placed in the collection that we know as the New Testament, his two volumes were separated: the first was placed with the gospels, and the second was left to pursue a career of its own. Not everyone, however, agrees with this analysis. We have no sure evidence that the two books were ever regarded as parts of a single work in the early church or that they were ever circulated as such.

Although most scholars are now willing to speak of the "unity of Luke-Acts," they may use that phrase with different levels of unity in mind. Mikeal Parsons has noted at least five such levels: authorial, theological, narrative, generic, and canonical.[3] Scholarly perceptions concerning these levels of unity might be plotted along a continuum: virtually everyone recognizes authorial unity (the two works have the same author) and virtually everyone accepts the lack of canonical unity (the two works are separated in modern Bibles). The other levels of unity are the areas where discussion is taking place.

Do Luke and Acts evince a *theological* unity? Robert O'Toole believes they do. In an appropriately titled monograph, *The Unity of Luke's Theology*, O'Toole argues that the two books present a cohesive theological theme when read together as a single entity.[4] The unifying theme is that God, who brought salvation to Israel, continues to bring salvation to Christians through Jesus Christ. The first volume describes the manner in which God provides salvation through Jesus; the second volume establishes Christians as the true Israel and, accordingly, as the recipients of this salvation. The point for our current discussion is that O'Toole believes these two works must be read together in order to understand Luke's theology: to consider one book without the other would only truncate Lukan thought.

Not all scholars envision such a close relationship. Stephen

Wilson, for instance, believes Acts was written many years after the gospel and addresses an entirely different set of concerns.[5] The book of Acts seeks to demonstrate that early Christians remained faithful to the Jewish law, but Luke was not particularly concerned about Jesus' attitude or practice regarding the law in his gospel. The reason for this shift in emphasis, Wilson theorizes, is that by the time Acts was written, Jewish (or possibly Jewish-Christian) attacks on Paul had necessitated a defense of Christianity on this point. At any rate, the shift in the place that an understanding of the law occupies in Luke's theology from one book to the next is evidence that both the gospel and Acts must be treated separately, as writings addressed to different occasions. In taking this approach, Wilson demonstrates that he does not assume theological unity of Luke-Acts to the extent that O'Toole does.

Similar disagreements occur when it is asked whether Luke and Acts evince a *literary* or *narrative* unity. Cadbury himself claimed that the two should be read as "a single continuous work." The book of Acts should not be regarded as "an appendix" or "an afterthought," but as "an integral part of the author's original plan and purpose."[6] More recently, Charles Talbert has presented evidence to support this thesis. In *Literary Patterns, Theological Themes, and the Genre of Luke-Acts*, he calls attention to recurrent patterns of parallelism between the two works.[7] Both works begin with a preface (Luke 1:1–4; Acts 1:1–5). In the gospel, the Spirit descends on Jesus as he prays (3:21–23); in Acts, the Spirit comes to the disciples who are also praying (2:1–13). Both Jesus and the disciples begin their ministries with sermons that focus on the theme of fulfillment of prophecy (Luke 4:16–30; Acts 2:14–40). Both books contain stories of lame men being healed (Luke 5:17–26; Acts 3:1–10) and stories about conflicts with religious leaders (Luke 5:29—6:11; Acts 4:1—8:3). In both, there are accounts of a centurion inviting the principal character to his house (Luke 7:1–10; Acts 10) and in both there are stories involving a widow and a resurrection (Luke 7:11–17; Acts 9:36–43). Both include reports of missionary journeys to the Gentiles (Luke 10:1–12; Acts 13–20) and both conclude with a prolonged account of a journey to Jerusalem where the hero is arrested on false charges (Luke 9:51—19:28; Acts 19:21—21:17).

Similarities between what happens in Jerusalem to Jesus (in the gospel) and to Paul (in Acts) are pronounced. Both receive an initially good reception (Luke 19:37; Acts 21:17–20a), enter the temple with a friendly attitude (Luke 19:45–48; 21:26), encounter hostile Sadducees but receive support from scribes (Luke 20:27–39; Acts 23:6–9), break bread and give thanks at a sacred meal (Luke 22:19a; Acts 27:35), and are finally seized by angry mobs (Luke 22:54; Acts 21:30). In the gospel, Jesus is slapped by the high priest's assistants (22:63–64) and in Acts, Paul is slapped at the high priest's command (23:2). Ultimately, both Jesus and Paul are brought to trial four times and are declared innocent three times (Luke 22:26—23:13; Acts 23—26). Both are rejected by the Jews (Luke 23:18; Acts 21:36), though regarded favorably by centurions (Luke 23:47; Acts 27:3, 43). Finally, both the gospel and Acts conclude on positive notes regarding the fulfillment of scripture (Luke 24:45–47; Acts 28:23–28).

Talbert believes that elaborate parallels such as these may have served a variety of purposes. They may have been aesthetically pleasing, served as mnemonic devices, and helped to underscore for Luke the essential unity that he saw between the mission of Christ and the mission of the church. In any case, the parallels would only make sense if both the gospel and Acts were read together as a single work. They are evidence that Luke constructed his two-volume work with meticulous intentionality and forethought, and that he did so under the assumption that the two parts would be compared to each other.

Robert Tannehill also believes Luke and Acts are intended to be read together. In *The Narrative Unity of Luke-Acts*, he attempts to demonstrate that Acts is a continuation of the gospel story.[8] Acts does not tell a related, but independent story, but completes the story begun in the gospel. Without Acts, the gospel of Luke would be incomplete, and without the gospel, Acts would be misunderstood. Promises made in the gospel are fulfilled in the book of Acts (e.g., cf. Luke 21:15 with Acts 6:10). Even promises that are *not* fulfilled provide a context for interpreting what happens in Acts. The gospel contains numerous predictions regarding the joyous salvation that God is bringing to all humanity. These projections are offered by reliable characters, including angels (1:13–17, 30–

37) and divinely-inspired prophets (1:46–55, 67–74; 2:29–35, 38). Quotations from scripture that point to the same thing are also recalled (3:4–6; 4:18–19). In Acts, however, Israel rejects Jesus and so Paul turns to offer God's salvation to the Gentiles (13:46; 18:6, 28:28). Apart from the promises of God revealed in Luke's gospel, a reader of Acts might conclude that it was God's will to transfer salvation from the Jews to the Gentiles. When Luke and Acts are read together, however, it becomes clear that the Jewish rejection of Jesus is an affront to God's plan, which remains, even at the end of the story, salvation for *all* humanity (see below, pp. 103–05).

Not all scholars are convinced by these arguments. Stephen Moore believes that contending for narrative unity for either of these documents, much less for both together, causes one to over-look the fact that both books are actually edited collections of divergent source material.[9] James Dawsey does not think enough attention has been paid to stylistic differences between the two works.[10] Mikeal Parsons has examined the ascension narratives that conclude the first volume (Luke 24:50–53) and open the second (Acts 1:6–11) and he believes these serve to separate the two as independent though interrelated works.[11]

Narrative unity, then, like theological unity, remains a topic for scholarly disagreement, even though all agree that both of these books were produced by the same person. The same can also be said for what is called "generic unity": Do Luke and Acts be-long to the same genre of literature? Scholars have not been able to agree on this question, nor, for that matter, on the related question of to what genre the book of Acts belongs.

Genre

The ancient Greco-Roman world knew three principal forms of narrative prose: history, biography, and the novel. The book of Acts is perhaps the only work surviving from antiquity to have been ascribed to all three.[12]

David Aune, in his work *The New Testament in Its Literary Environment*, assigns Luke-Acts to the genre of general history.[13] This type of literature typically narrated significant historical experiences of a particular ethnic or national group from their origin to the present. Many such histories were written by "barbarian" intellectuals during the Hellenistic period in attempts to communicate the achievements of their particular native lands. Aune suggests that, in adopting this genre to tell the story of the early church, Luke is conceptualizing Christianity on analogy to an ethnic group. He presents Christianity as a religious movement independent of Judaism and identifies Christians as a distinct group in their own right, worthy of historical treatment. Thus, his project provides the Christian movement with definition, identity, and legitimation.

Aune points to many similarities between Luke's writings and examples of Hellenistic historiography. The use of historical prefaces (Luke 1:1–4; Acts 1:1–5), the composition of speeches by principal characters, and the quotation of letters (Acts 15:23–29; 23:26–30) are standard conventions in such histories, intended to provide authenticity and verisimilitude. Likewise, Luke tends to avoid digressions, prizes eyewitness testimony as the most reliable evidence (Luke 1:2; Acts 1:3, 21–22), and uses rhetorical conventions to organize his episodes dramatically. All these are features of Hellenistic history writing that can be recognized in the works of such masters as Herodotus, Polybius, Lucian, and Josephus.

What Aune considers "general history" is only one type of historical writing in the ancient world. Other scholars have thought that Acts better fits into the sub-genre of "historical monograph," that is, work that focuses on an important sequence of events during a restricted period of time.[14] Still others have suggested it be treated as "apologetic historiography," with more interest in articulating the antiquity of Christianity in order to safeguard its political standing than in touting its cultural achievements to impress intellectuals.[15] All these views, however, regard Acts as belonging to the basic genre of Hellenistic historiography. Luke is to be regarded as an ancient historian and his work must be interpreted and evaluated as a work of ancient history (see pp. 80–83 below). Indeed, Aune complains that Eusebius, who did not write until the fourth century, is often credited with creating the new genre of "church history." The honor for doing this, Aune believes, should properly be conferred on Luke.

Charles Talbert, in his book, *What Is A Gospel?*, argues that

Luke-Acts does not belong to the genre of history at all but, rather, to biography.[16] In fact, Talbert believes all four of our canonical gospels should be considered ancient biographies. In arguing this thesis, he emphasizes that biographical texts in antiquity often employed myth and sometimes performed cultic functions, as do our gospels. Luke-Acts conforms to a specific type of biography known as "succession narrative." This genre is best exemplified in an early third-century work by Diogenes Laertius, *Lives of Eminent Philosophers*. At least some of the biographies contained in Laertius' work exhibit a threefold development: first, the life of the philosopher is recounted; next, stories concerning the community created by this figure are recalled; and, finally, the doctrine of the school as it now exists is summarized. When the book of Acts is joined to the gospel of Luke, just this sort of biography emerges. Acts provides the latter two components, the narratives concerning the community created and sustained by Jesus and, in the apostolic speeches, a summary of Christian doctrine.

Talbert recognizes some distinctions between Luke-Acts and Laertius' *Lives*, but finds the similarities compelling. Luke certainly conceives of Jesus as more than a philosopher, but some of the philosophers in Laertius' work are also depicted as divine figures whose abiding significance is more religious than academic. Laertius wished to show where the true followers of this or that philosopher could be found today. Similarly, Luke continues his biography of Jesus with a succession narrative that establishes normative Christianity as that represented in the circles of Paul.

Richard Pervo, author of the monograph, *Profit With Delight*, rejects identification of Acts with the literary genres of history or biography.[17] Rather, the work is an ancient novel written to entertain its readers even as it edifies them. The title of Pervo's book is taken from a quote by the Roman poet, Horace, who advises writers to combine "profit with delight" in order to please their readers at the same time that they admonish them. Scholars have long recognized Luke's ability to do this, Pervo insists, while simultaneously chastising him for playing fast and loose with the facts. He possesses a "bewitching ability to foist upon his readers one inconsistency after another and convert the most dreary material into good reading." This talent causes him to be viewed as "bumbling and incompetent as an historian yet brilliant and creative as an author." He is considered more edifying than accurate, "well-intentioned, but dumb."

Pervo believes such ambiguous evaluations of Luke's writings derive from the false assumption that Luke intended his Acts to be read as history, rather than as popular "historical fiction." The book relates stories about real people in known or at least plausible settings, but its overriding concern is not with factual accuracy. Rather, Acts relates stories intended to frighten, amuse, excite and surprise, though always with the edifying purpose of demonstrating the superiority of virtue. Pervo notes the preponderance of episodes dealing with such themes as harrowing escapes from peril, travel to exotic locations, and the working of fantastic miracles. Palace intrigue, mob scenes, adventurous voyages and shipwrecks are all standard novelistic features. Humor and wit also abound, as do what Pervo regards as burlesque and rowdy episodes (5:17–25; 12:5–17; 16:16–18; 19:14–16; 19:21–20:1; 23:6–10). Such stories reveal a tendency of Luke in this book to ridicule rather than confute his opponents, a sign of popular theology at its most primitive level. Luke, then, is surely writing for the masses. Learned readers would be offended by his comparison of Peter to Socrates and by his tendency to treat insignificant happenings as world-changing events. Likewise, the benefits, attitudes and fortunes of ordinary people rarely qualify for inclusion in history, but such is the stuff of which popular fiction is made.

Scholars have long recognized the affinities between ancient novels and certain popular books that were produced by Christians in the second and third centuries. These "apocryphal Acts" tell of the adventures of various apostles in terms that are obviously fantastic and fictitious. Most scholars, however, have regarded our canonical book of Acts as set apart from these latter works. Pervo minimizes the distinctions and claims that Acts has more in common with the apocryphal works than it does with any canonical New Testament books. It is, for instance, the only New Testament book to include a number of "punishment miracles," in which divine power operates to bring retribution on the wicked (e.g., 5:1–11; 13:8–12). Pervo does not, however, think Acts is completely unhistorical or unworthy of canonical status. The book succeeds at what it intends to do. It relates novelistic tales about historical persons in ways that help to popularize the Christian message while also edifying those who accept it. Luke was a prophet who used the genre of historical fiction as a medium to share his message.

This debate over the appropriate genre for the book of Acts overlaps with the discussions mentioned earlier regarding the relationship of Acts to Luke's gospel. Both Aune and Talbert approach the question of genre with regard to "Luke-Acts" as a whole, while Pervo does not believe these two books must be considered together from the standpoint of genre.[18] He does not regard the gospel of Luke as an ancient novel or attempt to read Luke-Acts together in this way.[19] Both Aune and Talbert would consider this a major failing in Pervo's thesis: he treats Acts in isolation and ignores the fact that Luke and Acts are actually a single work in two volumes. From Pervo's perspective, however, scholars such as Aune and Talbert operate from an unjustified *a priori* assumption: the search for a generic category into which both Luke and Acts can fit leads them to force one of the two works to conform to the pattern of the other.

Purpose

Questions concerning the literary genre of Acts and the relationship of this book to Luke's gospel are significant because they affect perceptions of the work's purpose.[20] A number of proposals have been made regarding Luke's purpose in composing Acts,[21] so many in fact, that a survey of them all could lead one to despair of ever finding the "right" answer. W. Ward Gasque, who has published such a survey, concludes that "it is impossible to isolate one exclusive purpose or theological idea which is the key."[22] Still, many of the ideas that have been suggested are not mutually exclusive: it is possible, even probable, that Luke wrote with more than one purpose in mind.

The most important theories regarding the purpose of Acts may be grouped into six categories: irenic, polemical, apologetic, evangelistic, pastoral, and theological.

1. *Irenic*. In the nineteenth century, F. C. Baur put forward a

theory about Acts that was to become one of the hallmarks of the famous "Tübingen school" of theology.[23] Baur believed that Acts was written to repair a major breach in early Christianity, a division that was rooted in the different expressions that had been given to the faith by Peter and by Paul. It is clear from other New Testament writings that Peter was recognized as a leader among Jewish Christians, while Paul became known as the "apostle to the Gentiles" (Gal 2:7). It is also clear that Peter and Paul did not always agree with each other or even get along with each other (Gal 2:11–14). By the time Acts was written, Baur theorized, the Petrine and Pauline parties in the church had become warring factions that threatened to split the new religion into two separate faiths. The book of Acts, then, was written to reconcile these factions and to restore unity to the church. Luke presents both Peter and Paul as heroes of the faith and, from the descriptions he gives, their approaches to ministry and theology appear to be quite compatible.

The consensus among modern scholars is that the situation of first-century Christianity was more complex than the Tübingen school envisioned. Many details of Baur's analysis of Acts have been rejected or revised. Still, the basic idea that Luke intended his book to help unify a church that was becoming increasingly diverse has stood the test of time. Paul Achtemeier, for instance, argues that Luke's idealistic portrait of a united church is more reflective of the "enormous desire within Christian community" for such unity than of actual historical circumstances.[24] The unity Luke describes is an ideal: if it was never a social and historical reality, it did exist in the hearts and minds of Christians who thought "this is how it *should* be." Luke's representation of the early church makes a theological statement that transcends contemporary concerns for accurate historical reporting.

2. *Polemical.* If the book of Acts can be read as an effort to smooth over differences between Christians, it can also be interpreted as an attempt to point out the differences between true Christians and those whom Luke considers to be heretics. Specifically, Acts has been regarded as an attack on Gnosticism, a religious ideology that sometimes infiltrated and threatened to undermine the orthodoxy of Christianity in its early years. Gnostics held,

for example, that Jesus was a purely spiritual being who was not truly human; they believed that human flesh and the material world itself were inherently evil.

Charles Talbert argues in his book, *Luke and the Gnostics,* that the book of Acts was intended to serve as a defense against Gnosticism in two ways.[25] First, as has been indicated previously (pp. 10–11), Talbert regards Acts as the latter portion of a two-volume biography of Jesus. The purpose of this latter portion is to indicate where the legitimate heirs of the Jesus tradition are to be found. Thus, the book of Acts tells the story of those persons who Luke regards as links between Jesus himself and the true followers of Jesus in Luke's own day. Leaders of Gnostic groups, who might claim that *they* are the real Christians, are ignored.

Second, Talbert finds numerous references in both Luke's gospel and the book of Acts that have an anti-Gnostic ring to them. For example, there is a tendency in Acts to avoid the terms "Christ" and "Christ Jesus" in favor of the simple proper name, "Jesus." Talbert thinks this is because the proper name emphasizes the humanity of Jesus (cf. Acts 2:22), while the christological titles were probably used by Gnostics who wished to accentuate his spiritual nature.

Talbert's argument for the purpose of Acts has not been refuted or rejected outright by scholars, but many are doubtful that the *primary* purpose of the book should be identified as a defense against Gnosticism. To some extent, the strength of Talbert's argument is tied up with his conception of Luke-Acts as a biography: those who accept his views concerning the literary genre of this book are likely to be the most attracted to his understanding of Luke's purpose.

Other proposals for polemical purposes behind Acts have also been suggested. Jack Sanders thinks Luke polemicizes against Jewish forms of Christianity (see below, pp. 68–69).[26]

3. *Apologetic.* Other scholars have described Acts as an attempt to defend the church from a force more worldly than Gnosticism: the Roman Empire. Scholars such as B. S. Easton and Ernst Haenchen have argued that Luke wrote the book of Acts in an effort to convince the Roman government that Christianity should be granted official status as a legitimate religion.[27] Accord-

ing to this theory, Judaism was a legally recognized religion in the Roman world, while Christianity was not. Luke, therefore, tries to demonstrate that Christianity is an outgrowth of Judaism (in fact, the true form of Judaism). Christians should not be persecuted, but should be granted the same legal sanctions as Jews.

One problem with this theory is that there is no sure evidence from the first century that Rome had a policy of classifying religions as legal or illegal. Still, many scholars would maintain that Luke is at least making overtures to Roman officials with the hope of improving relations between church and state (see below, pp. 72–73). He emphasizes the political innocence of Christians and seems intent on demonstrating that they are not politically subversive (Acts 18:14; 25:18; 26:32). Some scholars, however, doubt that Luke could have hoped for much success on this account. C. K. Barrett wonders whether any Roman official could have been expected to filter out "so much of what to him would be theological and ecclesiological rubbish in order to reach so tiny a grain of relevant apology."[28] For this reason, Paul Walaskay contends that the apology is actually directed to the church on behalf of the Roman Empire: Luke encourages Christians to view the empire positively and to strive to be good citizens (see below, pp. 72–73).[29]

Some scholars have suggested that Luke's apology does not concern the Roman Empire, but, rather, tensions between Christianity and Judaism. In *Luke-Acts and the Jews*, Robert Brawley argues that Luke responds to Jewish antagonism apologetically and proffers conciliation (see below, pp. 69–70).[30] In particular, Luke defends Paul and legitimates the Gentile mission that Paul has undertaken. The apology, then, is directed toward Jews who say Paul teaches apostasy and, perhaps, toward Jewish Christians who believe this. The view that Luke defends Paul for Jewish Christians who are "under fire from their Jewish neighbors" is argued more vigorously by Jacob Jervell in *Luke and the People of God* (see below, pp. 70–72).[31] Nils Dahl thinks it more likely that Luke is defending Paul for "God-fearing Gentiles at the fringe of the synagogue."[32]

4. *Evangelistic*. F. F. Bruce and J. C. O'Neill believe that Luke's purpose goes beyond apology.[33] Luke's desire with regard to the Roman world is not simply to dissuade pagans from persecut-

ing Christians; rather, Luke wants to convert them. This is why he tells the stories of the Roman proconsul Sergius Paulus (13:7–12) and of the jailer at Philippi (16:25–34), both of whom become Christians. Similarly, a direct evangelistic appeal is made to the Roman king, Agrippa (26:25–29). David Seccombe is more specific: Luke's emphasis on the proper use of possessions convinces him that Luke is writing evangelistically for people whose devotion to wealth might prevent them from accepting Christianity.[34]

Criticism of these theories, again, centers on the question of whether Luke really intends to address an audience outside the church. The majority of scholars believe that Luke's primary audience is not pagans but Christians. It is said that much of what he presents in his gospel and in the book of Acts would not be meaningful to outsiders. He presupposes, for instance, a solid grounding in the Old Testament and an acceptance of those writings as scripture. Theophilus, who is specifically addressed in Luke's prologues (Luke 1:3; Acts 1:1), is described as one who has been "informed" with regard to Christianity (Luke 1:4). It is debated whether this means that he has simply heard about the new religion or whether he has been formally catechized and is himself an adherent.[35]

5. *Pastoral*. If the book of Acts is addressed primarily to believers, then Luke's purpose may be to strengthen their faith and to offer them pastoral guidance. W. C. van Unnik describes the purpose of Acts as providing the "confirmation of the Gospel."[36] Building on this suggestion, Robert Maddox argues that Luke's purpose is to enable his readers to meet challenges that might cause them to doubt.[37] For example, many Christians in Luke's day may have wondered why, if Jesus was the Messiah, the Jewish people themselves had not recognized him as the one who fulfills their ancient prophecies. Luke writes to reassure these Christians that their faith in Jesus is not an aberration but, in fact, the goal toward which God's dealings with Israel were driving. Similarly, Philip Esler describes Luke's purpose as providing "political legitimation" for the Christian movement.[38] Luke presents Christians as good Roman citizens because he wants to show Romans who have become Christians that their faith in Jesus is not incompatible with allegiance to Rome. Once again, he must do this in the face of evidence to the contrary: the fact that Rome has not sanctioned the

new religion may have led some Roman Christians to question the legitimacy of the faith to which they have subscribed. Luke wants to reassure them that they did indeed make the right choice.

In developing these arguments, both Maddox and Esler focus on material in Acts that is apparently intended to defend the Christian faith or to encourage its acceptance. But they interpret this material as an appeal made to those who are already "within the fold." Even those who have been converted may continue to question the faith and entertain doubt. Luke's pastoral intention involves developing a witness that will address these concerns and confirm believers in their faith.

Other proposals for a pastoral purpose behind Acts have also been suggested. Robert Karris thinks Luke is concerned about assuring his community that God is faithful and that the promises of God will be fulfilled (see below, pp. 41–42).[39]

6. *Theological.* Hans Conzelmann identifies the main occasion for Luke's writings with a theological crisis in the life of the early church.[40] From Paul's epistles (e.g., 1 Cor 7:29–31), it appears that many of the early Christians believed the parousia, or second coming of Christ, was an event that was going to occur very soon. But this did not happen. As time passed and Jesus still did not come back, Christians had to reassess their beliefs about both the present and the future. Conzelmann believes Luke wrote his two-volume work as part of this theological enterprise. Luke shows himself to be a masterful theologian, able to reinterpret traditional thinking about eschatology and salvation history. According to Luke's vision, the period of Jesus' life on earth represented the "middle of time." As such, it was central to all history, but, just as it was preceded by a long "period of Israel," so it is to be followed by a lengthy "period of the church." The book of Acts was written to explain how this period of the church was inaugurated and to delineate what life and faith during such a time must be like.

Conzelmann's thesis, though very influential for a time, has found less acceptance in recent scholarship (see below, pp. 58–62).[41] Some scholars reject outright the notion that Luke abandoned hope for an imminent parousia; others question whether the realization that there might be a delay would have precipitated the sort of crisis Conzelmann imagines. Even those who find

Conzelmann's analysis of Luke's theology acceptable tend to disregard the notion that Luke's purpose in writing was to effect some grand reinterpretation of the faith. The book of Acts can be read as evidence that Christians in Luke's day were beginning to think differently about the future,[42] without it being assumed that Luke was consciously trying to get them to think that way.

Other theological motivations for the writing of Acts have been proposed. I. H. Marshall believes Luke and Acts were written to present a particular view of salvation (see below, pp. 48–50).[43] Paul Schubert and others have seen Luke's purpose as being to interpret God's plan as revealed in the Old Testament according to a scheme of "proof from prophecy" (see below, pp. 40–41).[44] Another prominent alternative to Conzelmann's salvation history model in recent scholarship has been what is called the "promise and fulfillment" motif. Advocates of this approach are apt to see Luke's purpose in writing as being to proclaim the certain fulfillment of God's promises (see below, pp. 41–42).[45] Although these various schools of thought emphasize different theological themes, they all regard Luke's purpose in writing Acts as the intentional promulgation of a particular theological concept.

Observations and Conclusions

The matters discussed in this chapter are basic for the study of Acts. If scholars disagree on the exact relationship that Acts bears to Luke's first volume, on the literary genre to which Acts should be ascribed, and on the purpose for which Acts was written, then it should not be surprising to find disagreement on other aspects of the interpretation of this book as well. In fact, the stances described in this chapter form the bases for many other ideas that will be discussed in the chapters that follow.

If the diversity of opinion seems overwhelming at this point, it may be helpful to note the areas on which there is widespread agreement. Contemporary discussions on the unity of Luke-Acts involve questions that might be described as "fine-tuning." Virtually everyone agrees that the two works have the same author and that they must, in some sense, be discussed together. Fifty years ago, even these propositions would have been subjects for much debate. Gasque, in his history of the interpretation of Acts, calls the progress made on this issue "the primary gain" of recent scholarly studies.[46] Continued discussion as to just how far the unity of the two works should be pressed will no doubt bring further gains as well.

On the subject of literary genre, an increasing number of scholars are content to regard Acts as unique. Indeed, as Colin Hemer has said, "it is unclear to what extent any of the New Testament documents are self-conscious documents that make use of contemporary forms."[47] This is especially true of Acts, unparalleled even in the canon. The fact that this book has been ascribed to so many different genres is testimony to the likelihood that it will not fit perfectly into any of them. It is possible, however, to note certain affinities that Acts has with other ancient works without insisting that the book meet all the literary expectations of those works.

On the question of purpose, it has been suggested that the various proposals should be considered, where possible, as complementary. As one scholar has noted, "any story that can be easily collapsed into one abstract idea or one specific purpose is not a very good story."[48] Whatever else it may be, the book of Acts is definitely a good story! We should be careful, therefore, not to reduce it to a one-factor analysis. Rather, we should read this book for what it is: a story "as complex and rich, as varied and mysterious, as true as life itself."[49]

2
The Composition of Acts

The book of Acts is perhaps the most readable book in the New Testament. Its lively style and inviting structure make it a favorite even among first-time Bible readers. The flow of the narrative is generally easy to follow. From a literary perspective, it is one of the best written books in the Bible.

This chapter will examine the text of Acts itself and will take note of the stylistic and structural characteristics that make this work so distinctive. In addition, some attention will be paid to the process by which the work must have come into being: what sources did the author have at his disposal and how did he shape these into the document that exists today?

Text

We do not have Luke's original Greek manuscript for the book of Acts, but copies of it that were produced by Christians over the years. Examination of these ancient Greek manuscripts reveals that the book existed in two different versions. One set of manuscripts preserves what scholars call the "Alexandrian"[1] text of Acts, while a different set of manuscripts preserves what is called the "Western text" of Acts.

Ernst Haenchen lists some of the chief differences between these two text types:[2]

1. The Western text of Acts is almost ten percent longer than the Alexandrian text. It does not contain full stories or episodes that are lacking in the Alexandrian text, but is simply wordier throughout. Numerous words, phrases, and even whole sentences

occur in the Western text that are not found in the Alexandrian manuscripts.

2. The Western text explains matters that are obscure or confusing in the Alexandrian text. For example, the Alexandrian text describes Peter and John as entering the temple in 3:8 and then mentions people running up to them in Solomon's Portico in 3:11. An uninformed reader might get the wrong impression that Solomon's Portico lies inside the temple. In the Western text, an intervening sentence informs the reader that Peter and John had gone back out of the temple before the people gathered.

3. The Western text makes more use of titles and pious language than the Alexandrian text. Passages that simply refer to "Jesus" in the Alexandrian text refer to "the Lord Jesus Christ" in the Western manuscripts.

4. The Western text exhibits a harsher attitude toward the Jews than is found in the Alexandrian text. Eldon Jay Epp, in a monograph on this subject,[3] observes that the Western text portrays the Jews and their leaders as more hostile toward Jesus and assigns to them greater responsibility for his death. Similarly, the Western text portrays the Jews as more hostile toward the apostles and as persecuting them more vigorously. At the same time, the positive response of Jews to the gospel is minimized in the Western text, as is the importance of Jewish institutions, customs, and practices. The church appears to be more Gentile and there is greater emphasis on those aspects of Christianity that differentiate the new faith from Judaism, such as the doctrine of the Holy Spirit.

At least some of the differences between these two text types are theologically significant. In Acts 15, the Alexandrian text records a decision that Gentile Christians will be asked to abstain from four things: idolatry, blood, anything strangled, and unchastity. Many interpreters believe the first three of these restrictions refer to dietary regulations: Gentile Christians are asked not to eat food offered to idols, food with blood in it, or meat from animals that have been strangled. In the Western text, however, the prohibition against "anything strangled" is missing and, in its place, is a decree to refrain from doing to another what you would not want done to you. This negative version of the golden rule casts the entire set of decrees in a moral light: the reader of the Western text would probably interpret the prohibitions against idolatry and blood in a moral sense also, that is, as decrees to abstain from *worshiping* idols or from *shedding* blood. Thus, the Western text presents the four restrictions placed on Gentile Christians in a way that avoids any reference to Jewish dietary laws.

At one time, it was thought that Luke might have published his book in two different editions,[4] but the contradictions that exist between the two versions make this seem unlikely. Today, most scholars believe the Western text represents a redaction of Acts, that is, a version of the book that has been subjected to editorial revision. Early in the life of the church, some person or persons sought to improve what Luke had written by adding explanatory comments, pious phraseology, and pro-Gentile (as well as anti-Jewish) remarks. Accordingly, the Alexandrian text is more representative of Luke's original work.

The Western text of Acts is nevertheless important to scholarship. Its very existence tells us something about the way Acts was regarded in the early church. Apparently, Acts was not accorded the same status as the gospels. Martin Dibelius suggests that Luke's gospel, accepted early as sacred scripture, was taken into the care of the church where efforts were made to preserve the text as faithfully as possible. But Acts, Dibelius continues, seems to have remained on the general market for a time, where copyists had no reason to regard the text as inviolate.[5]

The Western text of Acts is also important to scholars because in some individual instances it may preserve the more original reading.[6] Even if the Western text is a redaction, the manuscripts used by the redactors were probably older than any available to us today.[7] Besides, there is no way to be certain that the Alexandrian text type has not been redacted as well. For this reason, Bible translators usually do not follow either text type slavishly, but decide each verse on a case by case basis. Bruce Metzger has published *A Textual Commentary on the Greek New Testament*, which lists all of the significant options for each verse in Acts and then gives the opinion of a committee of translators as to which text seems best and why.[8] Most of the time, the committee decides in favor of the Alexandrian text, but occasionally the reading of the Western text is preferred.

Language and Style

When the gospel of Luke and the book of Acts are considered together, it becomes apparent that Luke employs the most extensive vocabulary of any writer in the New Testament. His books contain some 750–800 words that are not found anywhere else in the New Testament, a feature that makes them somewhat infamous among beginning Greek students.

From time to time, scholars have pointed to the richness of Luke's vocabulary in order to support some hypothesis about the author. The most famous such theory was that Luke's use of "medical terms" indicates the author must be a physician.[9] Henry Cadbury, however, demonstrated that Luke has an equal grasp of legal terminology and of nautical language, though no one has proposed the author must therefore be a lawyer or a ship captain. Luke's vocabulary, Cadbury concluded, proves only that he is well-educated.[10]

Luke's versatility with language is also evident in the varieties of style[11] found in his work. At times, Luke writes in what would be considered good Greek, with all the refinement of classical oratory. He uses the optative mood, rare elsewhere in the New Testament, and evinces a fondness for rhetorical devices such as littotes, by which an expression is emphasized through the negation of its opposite (e.g., "no small stir," 12:18). At other times, however, Luke writes in what is called "Semitic Greek": the Greek language is employed, but words or phrases are constructed according to the conventions of Hebrew or Aramaic grammar. This style may have appeared unrefined to anyone impressed by the more developed style used elsewhere.

These differences in style have been explained as deriving from the different sources that Luke might have used in the composition of his work (see below, pp. 27–30). Most modern scholars, however, regard the variety of style as deliberate on Luke's part. Cadbury suggests that Luke's use of Semitic Greek is intended to recall the language of the Septuagint, a Greek translation of the Old Testament that was widely used in Luke's day.[12] Luke writes portions of his narrative in language that sounds "biblical" to his readers. A modern analogy would be *Pilgrim's Progress* by John

Bunyan, which consciously imitates the literary style of the King James Version of the Bible.

Cadbury observes that in Acts, however, this Semitic biblical style is strongest when the narrative deals with what is happening in Palestinian circles. The more formal Greek is used after chapter 15 when the story moves out into the Greco-Roman world. Other scholars have noted similar tendencies: Haenchen observes that the very best, most literary style of Greek is used in Acts at precisely those places where the occasion would call for it: when Paul addresses the citizens of Athens (17:16–34), for example, or when he delivers an appeal to an important Roman official (24:1–23; 26:2–29).[13]

In short, Luke appears to have consciously constructed his narrative so that the style of language fits the occasion. This sort of literary artistry may be expected of writers today, but it was not an assumed standard in the first century. Such sensitivity to style is not, for instance, evident in any of the other three gospels. A century after Luke's time, the Roman writer, Lucian, had to instruct would-be authors: "If a person has to be introduced to make a speech, above all let his language suit his person and his subject" ("How To Write History," 58). This appears to be a lesson that Luke had learned.[14]

Structure

Studies on the literary structure of the book of Acts usually try to outline the work in one of two ways, according to a geographical scheme, or according to formal patterns discerned within the text.[15]

An example of a geographical scheme is that proposed by J. C. O'Neill.[16] The book of Acts yields to a fivefold division: (1) 1:9—8:3; (2) 8:4—11:18; (3) 11:19—15:35; (4) 15:36—19:20; (5) 19:21—28:31. This outline is introduced by the words of Jesus quoted in 1:8, "You will be my witnesses in Jerusalem and in all Judea and in Samaria and to the end of the earth." The first division deals with the witness in Jerusalem, the second with the witness in Judea and Samaria, and the final three with the taking of the gospel to the rest of the world. The divisions within this final phase follow other significant developments: the break between the third and fourth sections is marked by the important Jerusalem Council and the fifth section begins with Paul making his fateful decision to return to Jerusalem and to go from there to Rome. O'Neill believes this outline reveals Luke's understanding of a significant geographical shift that is occurring in the Christian religion: Jerusalem is being left behind and Rome is coming to the fore. In Acts, Jerusalem is the center of mission, but Rome is the goal. Ultimately, Jerusalem rejects the gospel and the gospel moves outward to be accepted elsewhere.

Another approach to structure is taken by Charles Talbert, who calls attention to literary patterns in the book of Acts.[17] In chapter 1 of this book, it was seen that Talbert believes many of the accounts in Acts are related in a manner that deliberately parallels what is reported in the gospel (see above, pp. 7–8). Talbert also finds fairly elaborate sets of parallels within the book of Acts itself. If the book is divided into two parts, a loose parallelism of content and sequence can be observed between Acts 1—12 and Acts 13—28. For example: the special manifestation of the Spirit in 2:1–4 and the preaching that results from it (2:14–40) corresponds to the manifestation of the Spirit and preaching in 13:1–40; the healing of the lame man and the speech it inspires in 3:1–26 corresponds to the healing of the lame man and the speech in 14:8–17; the stoning of Stephen in 6:8—8:4 corresponds to the stoning of Paul in 14:9–23; Peter's mission to the Gentiles (10:1—11:18) and subsequent imprisonment (12:1–19) corresponds to Paul's mission to the Gentiles and imprisonment (13—28). Talbert also finds other sets of parallels between individual sections of Acts, such as between 1:12—4:23 and 4:24—5:42 and between 15:1—21:26 and 18:12—21:26. Unlike O'Neill's scheme, Talbert's analysis does not yield a neat linear outline for the entire book of Acts. Rather, it exposes concentric patterns by which overlapping and recurring themes are interrelated.

An elaborate approach to the structure of Acts conceived by M. D. Goulder attempts to take note of both the geographical outline and recurrent literary patterns.[18] In his book, *Type and History in Acts*, Goulder divides Acts into four main sections: an apostolic section (1:6—5:42), a diaconal section (6:1—9:31), a Petrine section (9:32—12:24), and a Pauline section (12:25—

28:31). Within these sections, cycles of events can be perceived that correspond to each other and also to the cycle of Jesus' ministry in the gospel. The first section yields three such cycles, the second and third sections embody one apiece, and the fourth offers four more. The cycles, furthermore, also exhibit typological correspondences to the Old Testament. A number of scholars have wondered whether the relationships Goulder perceives are not overly subtle. J. L. Houlden is representative in his observation that the incidents reported in Acts do, after all, "reflect a fairly narrow range of religious concerns and themes, and it is not surprising that these recur."[19]

Sources

Where did Luke obtain the information on which the book of Acts is based? Haenchen offers a few suggestions[20]: maybe he wrote letters to congregations in important areas asking them for information; maybe he requested Christians traveling to these locations to "glean for him whatever was still known of the old times"; maybe he even visited the key sites himself. But all of this is speculation. The fact is, Luke does not tell us how or where he got his information and his silence on this point is a frustration to modern scholars.

Numerous theories have been proposed regarding possible sources that Luke might have used in his composition of Acts.[21] A problem with many of these theories, Haenchen suggests, is that they often proceed from the assumption that Luke composed Acts in a manner analogous to his gospel. Most scholars believe that Luke possessed written accounts of the life of Jesus (including the gospel of Mark) which he edited to produce his own gospel. With regard to the book of Acts, however, we have no sure evidence that any other written accounts of the early church ever existed. Nevertheless, exegetes sometimes interpret accounts in Acts with reference to Luke's editorial activity, presuming that he is redacting some preexisting document.[22] It is not impossible that Luke did have some written materials at his disposal, but care must be taken to determine the nature and extent of these sources. We will discuss representative theories for three different types of sources which have been discerned on the basis of three different types of evidence.

1. *An Aramaic source.* It was once suggested that the first part of Acts (e.g., chapters 1—12) was based on an early document that had been written in the Aramaic language. The primary evidence for this supposition was the noticeable Semitic style of Greek in which these chapters were written. Charles Cutler Torrey took this Semitic Greek as an indication that Luke had translated this portion of his narrative from an earlier Aramaic document.[23] Recent scholarship, however, has demonstrated the likelihood that Luke's "Semitic Greek" is an intentional stylistic device, adopted in conscious imitation of the Greek Old Testament (see above, pp. 24–25). This leaves Torrey's hypothesis without support.

Max Wilcox, on the other hand, does not believe the notion of Aramaic sources for Acts needs to be abandoned completely.[24] In his monograph, *The Semitisms of Acts*, Wilcox agrees that many of these Semitic expressions can be regarded as reflective of the Septuagint, but some, he holds, cannot. These latter, inexplicable Semitisms become "protruding elements" in Luke's narrative that may betray his reliance on sources. Such sources cannot be reconstructed; in most cases they were probably oral rather than written. They have been integrated so carefully into Luke's narrative that they are now barely detectable. The protruding Semitisms, however, offer at least a hint that Luke did not create his work out of nothing: they are "a sign to us of the authenticity and the antiquity of the material enshrined."

To leave the subject of sources only for a moment, Wilcox's study also casts an interesting sidelight on the problems involving the text of Acts discussed earlier in this chapter. Many of the Semitisms, it turns out, are found in the Western text of Acts, which is generally held to be inferior to the Alexandrian text type. Wilcox suggests that in places where such Semitisms occur, the antiquity of the Western reading should be given special consideration. It is in verses such as these that a case might be made for accepting the Western reading over the usually preferred Alexandrian text type.[25]

The results of Wilcox's study have been critiqued by Fred Horton.[26] The Semitisms in Acts that do not derive from imitation of the Septuagint, Horton believes, may simply reflect a form of Greek that was used in synagogues.[27] Accordingly, there is no cause to regard such expressions as reminiscent of more primitive sources. Likewise, the presence of Semitisms in the Western text does not commend the originality of its readings: if such expressions are reflective of "synagogue Greek," they could have been introduced by any Jewish-Christian group that had a copy of Luke's work.

2. *Local sources*. Adolf Harnack suggested another criterion for discernment of sources, namely, identification of the settings for the traditions that are related and of the persons in whom the traditions show particular interest.[28] He noticed, for example, that some of the material in Acts appears to have been written from the point of view of the church at Antioch (6:1—8:4; 11:19-30; 12:25—15:35). These Antioch traditions, he believed, had originally been concerned primarily with Stephen and Barnabas, though Luke himself has amended them to represent his own interest in Paul. Harnack also discerned a Caesarea tradition (3:1—5:16; 8:5-40; 9:31—11:18; 12:1-24), concerned primarily with Peter and Philip, and some Jerusalem material (12:1-47; 5:17-42), which is simply legendary. Harnack's theory has been subjected to numerous modifications and has prompted many counterproposals. The suggestion of an Antiochene source has fared the best over time and is still accepted (usually in some amended form) by many scholars today.[29]

3. *A travel diary*. A third approach to discernment of sources has utilized the methods of literary form criticism to detect different types of material that have been incorporated into Luke's narrative. Martin Dibelius believed that much of the latter portion of Acts reflects the literary form of an itinerary or travel diary.[30] He surmises that Luke possessed some document that listed the places Paul had visited, "which might well have been used on such journeys for the practical reason that, if the journey was made on another occasion, the route and the same hosts might be found again."[31] As evidence that Luke had such a record, he points to the numerous places mentioned in Acts where nothing is reported to have happened (e.g., 14:24-26; 17:1; 20:13-15). Since the mention of such places contributes nothing to the purpose of the narra-

tive itself, these references must be understood as derived from the source that Luke used.

Objections have been voiced to the idea of a travel diary. Some say the task would have been considered too expensive or too burdensome, especially for one who was expecting the world to end soon.[32] Others have wondered how such a diary could have survived the shipwreck at Malta (Acts 27:39–44). The proposal, however, has been helped by the research of Arthur Darby Nock, who has called attention to examples of such journals that are known to have existed in antiquity.[33]

Speeches

Out of about 1000 total verses in the book of Acts, over 300 constitute speeches delivered by various characters. These speeches are of different kinds. There are missionary speeches delivered to both Jews and Gentiles,[34] including Peter's sermon at Pentecost (2:14–36)[35] and Paul's discourse at Athens (17:22–31).[36] There are also defense speeches delivered by Paul at his various trials.[37] Other speeches are given to Christians by Peter (1:16–22; 11:15–17; 15:7–11) and by James (15:13–21), though the speech to Christians that attracts the most attention is Paul's farewell address to the Ephesian elders at Miletus (20:18–35).[38] The rather long speech by Stephen in 7:2–53 is also in a class by itself.[39]

In the first half of the twentieth century these speeches came to be considered the most important part of the book of Acts because they were thought to represent the actual content of the gospel proclaimed by the apostles. C. H. Dodd lay the foundation for this idea in his classic work, *The Apostolic Preaching and Its Developments*.[40] Although the book of Acts itself might have been composed fairly late, and although much of the narrative surrounding the speeches tends toward the legendary, the speeches are based upon material from the early church in Jerusalem. Luke remembered or had records of early Christian preaching around which he shaped stories about the early church. Whatever one thinks of the stories, the speeches preserve the *kerygma* or essential content of the apostolic message.

Today most scholars think exactly the opposite: the speeches in Acts represent the portions of the book where Luke exercised his literary license most freely. He composed the speeches and inserted them at key points in order to present his own understanding of how the events he reports should be interpreted. The movement toward this conception of the speeches was spearheaded by Martin Dibelius in his influential essay, "The Speeches in Acts and Ancient Historiography."[41] Dibelius notes that it was typical for historians in antiquity to compose speeches in order to present their own point of view. This appears to have been the case with Acts, for the literary style of all the speeches is the same, regardless of who is speaking. The missionary speeches, in particular, all follow the same pattern of presentation: a) an introduction regarding the particular situation; b) an account of Jesus' ministry, death and resurrection; c) citation of proofs or confirmation from the Old Testament; d) a call to repentance. In addition, it has been noted that the theology attributed to Paul in his speeches does not concur with what we know of Paul's theology from his own letters[42] (see below, pp. 35–36, 91–93).

Dibelius' view that the speeches in Acts are Lukan compositions is definitely the majority position today. In fact, whereas Dibelius was willing to grant that the speeches retain elements of ancient tradition, the trend in recent scholarship has been toward regarding them as totally free creations. F. F. Bruce and W. Ward Gasque remain the primary advocates of an historical basis for the speeches.[43] They note, for instance, that although the speeches are all similar linguistically ("Peter speaks like Paul and both speak like Luke"[44]), there are differences in theology or content. It is Paul who Luke represents as saying that believers are "justified" (13:39), using a term that we know was paramount in the historical Paul's vocabulary but which is never used by anyone else in Acts. Similarly, the speeches sometimes employ christological concepts not found elsewhere in Acts (see below, pp. 42–43). Thus, Bruce says, the speeches "express a diversity of viewpoints, including some at variance with the author's own." While ultimately composed by the author of Acts, they "were not composed by him out of whole cloth."[45]

The best light in which to view the speeches in Acts may be provided by a famous quote from the Greek historian Thucydides,

who wrote a *History of the Peloponnesian War* about 500 years
before Luke wrote Acts. Thucydides tells us that "with reference
to the speeches in this history . . . it was hard to record the exact
words spoken, both in cases where I was myself present, and where
I used the reports of others. But I have used language in accor-
dance with what I thought the speakers would have been the most
likely to say, adhering as closely as possible to the general sense of
what was actually spoken" (1.22).

Bruce, Gasque, and Dibelius all refer to this quote, for it
seems to express what must also have been Luke's intention.[46]
Disagreements occur primarily as to the extent to which Luke was
able to present "what was actually spoken" as opposed to what he
"thought the speakers would have been the most likely to say." All
seem to agree, however, that the speeches were given their current
form by Luke and so may be regarded as representative of his
concerns. For this reason, they remain primary resources for understanding the theology of the third evangelist.

On rhetorical features of the speeches, see pp. 97–99.

Authorship and Date

Scholars agree that the author of Acts is the same person who
wrote what is called "the gospel according to Luke." Both of these
works, however, are anonymous; their ascription to Luke is based
on an old church tradition[47] that they were written by "Luke the
physician, a companion of Paul," who is mentioned in such New
Testament passages as Colossians 4:14, Philemon 24, and 2 Timothy 4:11.

Is this tradition correct? Scholars have marshalled arguments
for and against it. Henry Cadbury, we have seen, produced a disser-
tation that destroyed the argument that medical language in these
writings proves the author was a physician.[48] In later years,
Cadbury's students are said to have joked that their mentor earned
his doctorate by taking Luke's away from him. The real issue,
however, is not whether the author of these writings was a physician or even a man named "Luke," but whether he was a companion of Paul. If it could be established that the third gospel and the
book of Acts were written by one of Paul's coworkers, most schol-

ars would agree that Luke is as likely a candidate as any. The tradition could be accepted.

At first glance, it appears that the author of Acts *claims* to have been a companion of Paul. In certain passages (16:10–17; 20:5–15; 21:1–8; 27:1—28:16), he uses the pronoun "we" in a way that implies he is with Paul on those occasions. All of these passages occur in the portion of Acts that form critics believe is taken from a travel diary. Dibelius had no trouble believing that the diary is one Luke himself may have kept.[49] Others, however, think the author of Acts has simply acquired such a diary and so is able to make use of it without ever having been a companion of Paul himself.[50]

Jacques Dupont has problems with this latter view.[51] In his book, *The Sources of Acts*, he notes that the vocabulary, style, and theological interests of the "we sections" are consistent with those of the book of Acts as a whole. If the author is using a source preserved by another, he has completely reworked it. Is it really very likely that a writer who edits his material so thoroughly would simply copy the inappropriate "we" into his text? Dupont thinks not. Overliteral transcription is not this author's way of dealing with a source. The "we" is present deliberately, because the author wishes it to be understood that he took part in the events he is recounting.

A monograph by Jürgen Wehnert, however, supports the idea that the "we" in these passages can be attributed to a Pauline companion other than the author.[52] Luke retains the first-person plural precisely because it authenticates what he is reporting as the account of an eyewitness. Wehnert points to examples of authors switching to "character narration" in Old Testament writings such as Ezra and Daniel.

Vernon K. Robbins has suggested another explanation for the "we passages."[53] He cites numerous examples to show that there was a "sea voyage" genre in first-century Greco-Roman literature and that this literature often employed the stylistic device of first person narration. There was a natural tendency for the author of Acts to narrate those portions of his work dealing with sea travel in the first person. Although it may seem strange to us, this was an accepted literary convention of the day.

Robbins also suggests another reason for the writer to have used such a device. At the beginning of his two-volume work, he tells Theophilus that the things about which he writes "have been accomplished among *us*" (Luke 1:1). By using the first person here, the author indicates that he feels he has in some sense participated in the events recounted in the gospel, even though he himself was not an eyewitness to them (cf. Luke 1:2–3). Similarly, the "we passages" in Acts convey the strong sense of union that this author feels with the early Christian leaders about whom he writes. His purpose in these passages is to explain how "we Christians" spread throughout the world. The "we" refers not just immediately to Paul and his companions but, ultimately, to the entire Christian church.

Joseph Fitzmyer raises some objections to Robbins' view in his book, *Luke the Theologian*.[54] First, he wonders why, if this is a studied literary device, it appears only where it does. Sea voyages are described in other places in Acts, where the device is not used. Second, he regards the equation of the "we passages" in Acts with sea-voyage literature as somewhat inexact, since at least some of the material in the "we passages" deals with events on land. Finally, Fitzmyer objects to several of the examples Robbins deduces as representative of a sea-voyage genre, though he does not question the existence of such a genre altogether. Taking these matters into consideration, Fitzmyer concludes that the best explanation for the "we passages" remains the supposition that they come from a record that the author of Acts once kept when he traveled with Paul and which he has now incorporated into his narrative about those travels.

An even greater challenge to the tradition that Acts was written by a companion of Paul is posed by comparisons between the portrayal of Paul in Acts and the image of Paul derived from the latter's own writings. Haenchen lists discrepancies between the Paul of Acts and the Paul of the letters[55]: 1) in Acts Paul is portrayed as a great miracle worker, but in his letters Paul never mentions any of these remarkable deeds; 2) in Acts Paul is an outstanding orator, but in his letters Paul admits to being a feeble, unimpressive speaker (2 Cor 10:10); 3) in Acts only "the twelve" are truly apostles, but in his letters Paul insists that he is an apostle as well (Acts 1:21–23 gives qualifications for apostleship, in spite of 14:4, 14; cf. 1 Cor 15:5–8; Gal 2:1–10). To these points may be added the observation that Acts never portrays Paul as writing letters or, for that matter, gives any indication that its author had ever read any of Paul's letters.[56]

More serious discrepancies have been noted between the theology of Paul as expressed in Acts and that which we find in Paul's own letters. In an essay "On the 'Paulinism' of Acts," Philipp Vielhauer calls attention to four areas where he believes this is true[57]: 1) Acts presents Paul as telling pagans they possess a natural kinship with God which needs only to be purified, corrected, and enlarged (Acts 17:22–31); in his letters, Paul says pagans will suffer the wrath of God because their ignorance of God is without excuse (Rom 1:18–23). 2) Acts depicts Paul as espousing a positive attitude toward the Jewish law, which now needs only to be supplemented by faith in Christ (Acts 13:38–39); in his letters, Paul declares that the law has absolutely no saving significance for Jew or Gentile and he speaks of Christ as "the end of the law" (Rom 10:4). 3) In Acts, Paul speaks of the crucifixion of Jesus as an error of judgment and as a sin of the Jews without ever mentioning its significance for salvation (Acts 13:27–30); in his letters, Paul speaks of the cross as judgment upon all humanity but also as God's saving act that effects reconciliation (Rom 5:6–11; 2 Cor 5:14–21). 4) In Acts, Paul speaks of the return of Christ only in a peripheral way (Acts 17:30–31); in his letters, Paul makes it clear that he lives in expectation of an imminent parousia and it is this expectation that motivates his mission and determines his relationship with the world (1 Cor 7:29–31).

Vielhauer's essay has had a controversial reception. Haenchen considers it a major breakthrough, representative of a new approach to Lukan theology.[58] Gasque, however, has this to say: "It would be difficult to find a better example of allegedly critical research to illustrate the dangers of a false critical methodology and theological bias."[59] The tenor of such comments may be determined by what is at stake: if Vielhauer's analysis is correct, then Acts may have been written by a person who was quite ignorant of what Paul really believed or even by someone who intentionally misrepresented those beliefs.

Joseph Fitzmyer is willing to grant that the author of Acts misrepresents Paul at times, but he does not think this rules out the possibility that the author could have been one of Paul's companions.[60] A careful study of the "we passages," Fitzmyer says, reveals that the author would only have been with Paul when the latter traveled from Troas to Philippi (16:10–17), from Philippi to Jerusalem (20:5–15; 21:1–18), and from Caesarea to Rome (27:1—28:16). Apparently, the author stayed in Philippi during the time covered by 16:18—20:4. When the events reported in this portion of the narrative are matched to our best chronology of Paul's life, it becomes evident that this intervening period lasted for about eight years. This, furthermore, was the period of Paul's life when he encountered opposition from Judaizers and had to deal with the charismatic factions in Corinth, events that were instrumental in shaping his theology. It was also the time when he wrote most of his important letters. It is not inconceivable, Fitzmyer concludes, to believe that the author of Acts was a "sometime companion" of Paul who may not have fully understood Paul's theology or, for that matter, have been fully committed to preserving Paul's theology intact.

Vielhauer's contention that Luke misrepresents Paul raises other important questions for the study of Acts (see below, pp. 91–94). Fitzmyer's work, however, suggests that this charge does not in any case preclude acceptance of the tradition that the work was produced by one of Paul's traveling companions, most likely the one we know today as "Luke."

When was the book of Acts written? The evidence is inconclusive. Since the book mentions Paul's arrival in Rome (c. A.D. 56), but not his death (A.D. 64), a few scholars have suggested it was written during the interim between these two events, or around A.D. 60.[61] Against this theory is the likelihood that Luke's gospel was written after the fall of Jerusalem in A.D. 70 (cf. Luke 21:20) and that Acts was probably written later than the gospel.[62] On the other hand, Acts had to have been written at least by A.D. 150, since we have explicit references to it in other literature not much later than that.[63] An occasional scholar will argue that it was written almost that late.[64] Against such a view is the puzzle of why the author would not exhibit greater knowledge of Paul's letters if he were writing at such a late period. The great majority of scholars date Acts somewhere around A.D. 80–85, with the admission that this cannot be established with precision.

Observations and Conclusions

This chapter has attempted to describe some of the problems and questions that scholars face when they try to reconstruct the process by which Acts was written. One tension that has run throughout these discussions concerns the question of what should be attributed to the evangelist's sources and what should be credited to his own literary skill. Are the Semitisms in Acts evidence that the author is drawing on primitive tradition or are they conscious imitations of the linguistic style used in the Septuagint and in the synagogue? Are the speeches a testimony to authentic apostolic tradition or to the author's own compositional skill? Do the "we passages" derive from a travel diary or are they a literary device employed by the author?

Another example of such a tension, not discussed in the material above, concerns the presence of doublets in Acts: Luke has two accounts of the conversion of Cornelius (10:1–48; 11:1–18) and three reports of Paul's experience on the road to Damascus (9:1–19; 22:4–16; 26:9–18). Some scholars have taken the presence of these repetitive accounts as an indication that Luke has more than one report of these events in his sources.[65] Others view the use of repetition as a characteristic of the writer's literary style (see below, pp. 102–03).[66]

In some sense, this tension between attributing facets of the text to Luke's sources or to Luke's style corresponds to the different views concerning the genre and purpose of Acts discussed in the last chapter. Scholars who tend to view Acts as a work of history will naturally focus their research on the question of sources, while those who view the book as a work of literature will be more interested in the author's stylistic devices. Both of these approaches to Acts will be discussed more fully in chapters 5 and 6.

3
The Theology of Acts:
God, Jesus, and the Holy Spirit

The title given to Luke's second book, "Acts of the Apostles," is misleading. Peter is the only one of the twelve apostles whose exploits are recounted in any detail. Even if Paul is to be thought of as an apostle in some secondary sense (14:4, 14), his adventures are not really the focus of this book either. Rather, it is *divine* acts with which Luke is ultimately concerned. Everything that Luke recounts has theological significance. Accordingly, the bulk of scholarship devoted to his writings has attempted to interpret them in terms of their theology.

God

Defining Luke's concept of God is not as simple as might be supposed.[1] Very little in the book of Acts describes God's attributes outright. What Luke believes about God is largely assumed within the narrative and must be discovered by paying careful attention to its distinctive features. For example, the book of Acts contains stories in which God kills people (5:1–11; 12:21–23; possibly 1:18) that would seem right at home in the historical books of the Old Testament. Does Luke retain this notion of God as one who brings swift retribution upon the wicked to a degree that other New Testament writers do not?

Or, again, Luke displays a penchant for the title, "Most High God," which he uses twice in the book of Acts (7:48; 16:17) and five times in his gospel (1:32, 35, 76; 6:35; 7:48; 8:28). This title was used for God in the Septuagint and other Jewish writings but was also used in the Greek world for pagan deities such as Zeus. As such, the term might have had a special appeal for pagan converts to Christianity.[2] But in what sense does Luke use the term and how does he wish it to be understood?[3]

The matters just mentioned concern minor elements in Luke's narrative on which scholarly discussion has been limited. Two aspects of Luke's concept of God, however, appear to be intrinsic to the entire work and have been the focus of much study.

1. *God controls history.* For Luke, God is the lord of history. God determines what will happen, as well as when, where, and how it will happen. God is in charge.

In *The Unity of Luke's Theology*, Robert O'Toole calls attention to Luke's frequent use of verbs that emphasize the foreknowledge, will, plan, or purpose of God.[4] God fulfills (*plēroō*) and brings to pass events predicted in the scriptures (Luke 1:20; 4:21; 21:24; 22:16; 24:44; Acts 1:16; 3:18; 13:27; 14:26). God determines (*horizō*) the timetables and geographical boundaries of history (Acts 17:26) as well as the fate of individuals—including Jesus (Luke 22:22; Acts 2:23; 10:42; 17:31). Times and seasons are set (*tithēmi*) by God, as are the purposes for individual lives (Acts 13:47). God appoints (*tassō*) the temporal (Acts 22:10) and eternal (Acts 13:48) destiny of people.

The most important such verb that Luke uses is the little Greek word *dei*, which means "it is necessary" or "it must."[5] In Luke's writings, things frequently happen simply because they *must* happen. In the gospel, this is all the explanation needed for why Jesus sometimes does things that offend people (2:48; 19:7): he does what he must do (2:49; 19:5). This expression of divine necessity is linked in both the gospel and in Acts to the passion. It is necessary for Jesus to die and to rise from the dead (Luke 9:22; 13:33; 17:25; 24:7, 26; Acts 17:3). The same sense of divine necessity governs the actions of the early church in Acts. It is necessary for Judas to be replaced (1:22) and for Paul to visit Rome (19:21; 23:11; 25:10; 27:24). It is necessary for Christians to experience tribulations (14:22) and suffer for Christ's name (9:6; 16). It is necessary for the word of God, which ultimately goes to the Gentiles, to be spoken first to the Jews (13:46).

Luke's abundant use of *dei* and other terms expressing necessity indicates a profound sense of divine purpose. O'Toole believes this emphasis on God's purpose is also brought out by Luke's references to the fulfillment of scripture. Numerous events, including the passion and resurrection of Jesus (Luke 18:31–33; 20:17; 22:37; 22:69; 24:25, 27, 44; Acts 3:18), the outpouring of the Spirit on Pentecost (Acts 2:16–21) and the ministry to Gentiles (Luke 24:45–47; Acts 15:15–17; 28:25–28) have all been foretold in the Old Testament. Accordingly, these events are part of God's plan.

Descriptions of divine guidance likewise testify to the reality of God's plan. In Acts, God directs people through the Holy Spirit (8:29, 39; 10:19; 11:12; 13:2–4; 16:6–7; 19:21; 20:22–23, 28), prophets (11:28; 21:11), angels (5:19; 8:26; 10:3, 7, 22; 11:13; 12:7–15, 23; 27:23–24), and visions (10:3; 10:11–19; 11:5–10; 16:9–10). This continual guidance is evidence that God, who predestined what has happened up to now (Acts 2:23; 4:28), is still in control of what takes place.

In short, God is in charge of history and directs its course according to a divine plan. O'Toole goes on to inquire as to what this plan is. According to Luke-Acts, the plan of God is a plan of salvation. Luke's main theological theme concerns not just history in general but *salvation history*. Luke writes to show how God, who brought salvation to Israel in the past, continues to bring salvation to Christians in the present.

O'Toole's position, as stated, is not controversial. Virtually all Lukan scholars would agree that the book of Acts exhibits strong interest in God as the director of salvation history. The disagreements occur when scholars attempt to define Luke's concept of God's plan with more precision. Hans Conzelmann, for instance, proposes that God is depicted as dividing history into three distinct eras: a time of Israel, a time of Jesus, and a time of the church (see below, pp. 58–59).[6] Others believe Luke thought more in terms of two periods: a time of prophecy and a time of fulfillment.[7]

2. *God makes promises and keeps them.* Another aspect of Luke's concept of God is deduced from the strong emphasis on promise and fulfillment in his writings. Much of the data relevant to this point is the same as that discussed above, particularly the repeated references in Luke and Acts to fulfillment of scripture.

But now a broader interpretation is given to this data: the Old Testament passages that Luke considers to be fulfilled by New Testament events were not simply predictions—they were promises. Their fulfillment is testimony not only to God's sovereignty, but also to God's faithfulness. The principal exponent of this view has been Robert Karris, but his work is best understood against an historical backdrop of other studies.

In the 1950s a number of Lukan scholars developed a paradigm for understanding Luke-Acts according to a "proof-from-prophecy" motif.[8] This approach understood Luke's purpose in emphasizing the fulfillment of Old Testament scriptures as mainly apologetic. Luke indicates that the events he reports were prophesied in the Old Testament because he thinks this proves the events are part of God's plan. In particular, Luke cites what he regards as messianic prophecies fulfilled by Jesus in order to prove that Jesus is the Messiah. This proof-from-prophecy school suffered a major setback in 1969 with the publication of Martin Rese's *Alttestamentliche Motive in der Christologie des Lukas*.[9] Rese examines Luke's Old Testament citations in detail, but finds no evidence of an apologetic motive behind any of them. Where a scheme of prophecy and fulfillment can be detected, the citation of the Old Testament passage serves to interpret or explain the meaning of the New Testament event rather than to establish its legitimacy. Sometimes, in fact, the process works in reverse: the New Testament event explains the meaning of the Old Testament passage, which otherwise would be obscure. This emphasis on a didactic rather than apologetic motive for Luke's linkage of scripture with contemporary events has been picked up and expanded by other scholars, including Eric Franklin and Darrell Bock.[10]

Karris, however, has revived the old proof-from-prophecy school with a new twist.[11] What Luke wishes to prove by emphasizing that prophecies made long ago are now being fulfilled is not so much the legitimacy of the prophecies or the events, but the faithfulness of the God who stands behind both. The simple fact that God makes and keeps promises is a point Luke considers worth establishing. The people for whom Luke was writing were troubled by questions such as these: Is God's love continuous? Has God been faithful to promises made to the Jewish people? Will God be faithful to promises made to Christians through Jesus?[12] The destruction of the Jewish temple by Rome and the failure of Christian missionary efforts to convert Jews to Christ might have called God's faithfulness to the so-called "chosen people" into question. Furthermore, Jesus had not yet returned as he had promised. In the face of such doubts, Luke found it necessary to emphasize that God had kept all promises made in the past and so could be counted on to keep all promises remaining for the future.

Jesus

The christology of Acts has been a popular subject in recent scholarship. Francois Bovon counts fifteen major monographs and over 150 articles on this subject between the years 1950–1975 alone.[13]

Different approaches are taken. One focuses on the various titles attributed to Jesus in Acts: Christ, Leader, Lord, Master, Prophet, Savior, Servant, Son of David, Son of God, Son of Man.[14] Another focuses on the different phases of Jesus' life as they are described in Acts: baptism, ministry, death, resurrection, ascension, parousia.[15] Yet another focuses on the overall structure of Luke-Acts and looks for models that describe the way Jesus is presented in both books: benefactor, immortal, philosopher, prophet.[16]

Different approaches naturally raise different questions and yield different results. In what follows, we will discuss some of the questions that have evoked the most comment in recent scholarship, with the realization that some of these are more pertinent for one approach to christology than for another.

1. *Is there a consistent christology in Acts?* Some scholars ask whether it is possible to speak of a "christology of Acts" at all. A number of exegetes have detected in this book a variety of different christologies, which they believe derive from Luke's use of various sources.[17] John A. T. Robinson, for example, claims that a unique understanding of Jesus lies behind the words Peter speaks in Acts 3:19–21: "The Lord may . . . send you the Messiah . . . Jesus . . . whom the heavens must receive until the time of restoration."[18] Robinson interprets these verses to imply that Jesus, al-

ready ascended into heaven, has not yet been sent to earth as the Messiah. Apparently, Robinson surmises, Luke drew these words from a source preserved by some groups of Christians in the early church. The idea reflected in this source, namely that Jesus would not be manifested as the Messiah until his second coming, is not found anywhere else in the book of Acts, or, for that matter, in the New Testament. The idea, Robinson concludes, was a very primitive way of thinking about Jesus that did not survive long. Most scholars, however, do not think Acts 3:19–21 rules out the possibility that Jesus has already come once as Messiah.[19]

Recent research on the composition of Acts indicates that the sources Luke used were carefully integrated into his narrative (see above, pp. 27–30). An astute exegete may discern words or phrases left over from the sources, but the theology of the work as a whole belongs to Luke. Even what is believed to derive from sources may be considered expressive of Luke's theology, for Luke did not retain what he did not personally favor. If this is true, then all of the christological material found in Acts can be taken as testimony to Luke's own christology. The fact that there is some diversity in this material indicates only that Luke's ideas are broadminded or undeveloped.

2. *Is the christology of Acts consistent with that of Luke's gospel?* In chapter 1 of this book, we indicated that scholars disagree as to the extent of theological unity that exists between Luke's two volumes (see above, pp. 6–7). This discussion often focuses specifically on issues of christology.

Some scholars point to inconsistencies between the way Jesus is described in the gospel and in Acts as evidence that the latter work preserves a christology essentially different from that of the gospel. In Luke's gospel, for example, the story of Jesus' career begins with his birth. In Acts, summaries of Jesus' career begin at the earliest with his baptism (e.g., 1:22; 10:37). Some scholars, such as John A. T. Robinson and Ferdinand Hahn, suggest that Acts preserves an "adoptionist" christology, by which Jesus is thought to have been adopted by God at his baptism or at some other significant juncture.[20] In fact, Acts 2:32–36 seems to suggest that God made Jesus Lord and Christ at his *resurrection*, a view quite different from that of the gospel, where Jesus is "Christ the

Lord" from birth (2:11). Other scholars note, however, that the birth story of Jesus is somewhat unique even within Luke's gospel. After the first two chapters, there are no further references (in the gospel or in Acts) to the remarkable circumstances of Jesus' birth. Furthermore, Acts 2:32–36 does not have to be interpreted as implying that Jesus was not the Lord or Christ before his resurrection. It may mean that the resurrection was the point at which his identity as Lord and Christ was verified or at which his destiny as Lord and Christ was fulfilled.[21]

An approach that has found more acceptance in recent years has been to identify differences between the descriptions of Jesus in the gospel and in Acts as serving some intentional function. C. F. D. Moule proposes in an article on "The Christology of Acts" that Luke speaks differently about Jesus in Acts than he does in the gospel in order to reflect the change in consciousness that occurred among Christians after the resurrection.[22] In the gospel Jesus is not referred to as the Lord, as the Son of man, or as the Son of God by human characters, but in Acts human beings use all these designations for him (10:36; 9:20; 7:56). In the gospel Jesus is called *a* prophet, but in Acts he is said to be *the* prophet expected in the last days (3:22–23; 7:37). In the gospel Jesus brings salvation to people (19:9–10), but in Acts it is stated that there is no salvation in anyone else (4:12). In short, the christology of Acts is more exalted than that of the gospel, a development that is logical, in light of the post-resurrection perspective that Acts intends to present.

Similar conclusions are reached by Darrell Bock in his study, *Proclamation from Prophecy and Pattern*.[23] Bock studies the way in which Luke uses Old Testament passages to elucidate who Jesus is. In the gospel, passages are cited that identify Jesus as a regal Messiah-Servant (e.g., Ps 2:7 and Is 42:1 in Luke 3:15 and 9:35; Is 61:1–2 and 58:6 in Luke 4:17–19; and Ps 118 in Luke 13:35, 19:38, and 20:17). In the latter part of the gospel, however, Luke introduces tensions into this portrait. Luke 20:42–43 cites Psalm 110 in a way that questions the sufficiency of identifying Jesus as a messianic Son of David. Luke 22:69 also alludes to Psalm 110 in portraying Jesus in more exalted terms than would be associated with the Messiah. In short, the gospel begins with a consistent portrayal of

Jesus as the Messiah but progressively introduces tensions that imply he is "more than a Messiah." These tensions are resolved in Acts, where Jesus is declared to be Lord as well as Messiah (Acts 2:21, 34–36). In fact, he is now proclaimed as "Lord of all" (Acts 10:36) and as "Judge of the living and the dead" (Acts 10:43).

Both Moule and Bock, then, identify the christology of Acts as more explicitly exalted than that of Luke's gospel, but both also explain this distinction as intentional and as consistent with Luke's overall purpose. Moule believes Luke wants to emphasize the resurrection as a watershed in christological consciousness. Bock sees Luke's purpose as more rhetorical: the evangelist leads his reader to an ever deeper understanding of Christ by progressively introducing more exalted categories of thought.

Finally, we should note that some scholars do not see any significant distinction between the way Jesus is presented in Luke's gospel and in Acts. Donald Jones maintains that the titles "Servant," "Christ," and "Son of God" are all used interchangeably by Luke and that Luke does not distinguish between an earthly Jesus in the gospel and an exalted Lord in Acts.[24] The most significant texts for Jones' argument are found, once again, in the gospel's infancy narrative (Luke 1—2), where Jesus is called "Lord" (1:43, 76) and Son of God (1:32, 35) even before his birth. Moule regards these verses as "exceptions" and Bock treats them as presenting "a foretaste" of Luke's later emphasis.

3. *Does Acts present Jesus as absent or present?* One of the most significant implications of Hans Conzelmann's model for Luke's understanding of salvation history is that it relegates Jesus and the salvation he brings to a period of past history (see above, pp. 18–19).[25] The parousia has been delayed and so the church must struggle theologically to define its role in the absence of its Lord. C. F. D. Moule also believes Acts presents Jesus as no longer on earth but in heaven, as exalted and as therefore temporarily absent.[26] Such thinking may be contrasted with the idea expressed in Paul's letters that the church represents Christ's body on earth (Rom 12; 1 Cor 12).

George MacRae modifies this notion of an "absentee christology" somewhat by noting four "modes of presence" through which Christians continue to relate to Jesus in Acts.[27] First, Jesus continues to guide his followers through the work of the Holy Spirit, who is even called the "Spirit of Jesus" at one point (16:7). Second, the name of Jesus is invoked continuously in Acts in a sense that conveys the reality and power of Jesus' presence; salvation (2:21; 4:12), healing (3:6; 6:18), and forgiveness of sins (10:43) are all mediated by this name. Third, Jesus is made present through the preaching of the gospel, the "message of salvation" (13:26). Finally, Jesus is present in the lives of his followers, who preach, work miracles, and even suffer in a manner analogous to him.

Gerhard Krodel does not think Acts represents Jesus as absent, except in the relatively insignificant sense of no longer being present in bodily form.[28] Luke regards God, who lives in heaven, as the one in whom we live and move and have our being (Acts 17:28). Similarly, Jesus can be seated at the right hand of God in heaven (7:56) and also remain active on earth. He appears to Saul on the Damascus road (9:4–5). When he speaks to Saul, furthermore, he asks: "Why are you persecuting *me*?" (9:5). Thus, Jesus identifies himself with the disciples whom Saul has persecuted (cf. Luke 10:16). Finally, Krodel notes that Luke begins the book of Acts by saying: "In the first book, I have dealt with all that Jesus *began* to do and teach." Now, in the second volume, Krodel surmises, Luke intends to deal with what Jesus *continues* to do and teach through the church.

Eventually, this argument turns on interpretation of an event unique to Luke's narratives: the ascension (Luke 24:50–51; Acts 1:9–11). For Conzelmann, the ascension is a departure: in telling this story, Luke marks the precise time when Jesus left the earth and so signals the beginning of the period of his absence.[29] Gerhard Lohfink agrees. In his detailed study, *Die Himmelfahrt Jesu*, he decides that the ascension is essentially a parousia in reverse.[30] Jesus leaves now, but will some day return. In the meantime, his followers are not to stand staring into heaven (Acts 1:11), but should use the time of the church constructively for mission.

Eric Franklin, however, interprets the ascension not as Jesus' departure but as his exaltation.[31] In his study, *Christ the Lord*, Franklin stresses that the ascension means Jesus is now enthroned in heaven, accessible through prayer and worship. Similarly, Robert Maddox views Jesus in Acts, not as a figure of the past, but as a living Lord.[32] Luke simply uses a different conceptual model for describing the relationship between Jesus and his followers than that used by other New Testament writers. Instead of an indwelling of Christ in the believer, Luke describes an ongoing vertical communication between the disciples on earth and the Lord who reigns in heaven. Though different, this model does not imply a weaker relationship.

4. *How does Jesus save?* There can be no doubt that Acts links Jesus with salvation (4:12; 16:31), but the details of this connection are not absolutely clear. Scholars have tried to define what Luke means by salvation and have offered explanations for the saving role that Acts attributes to Jesus.

The words "Savior" and "salvation," which are not used at all in Matthew or in Mark, are found eight times in Luke's gospel and nine times in the book of Acts.[33] The words may derive from either (or both) of two backgrounds. In the Greek world, salvation was typically associated with the bestowal of various blessings and gifts, while in the Old Testament it was conceived of more as deliverance from enemies.[34]

Frederick Danker thinks the Greek sense of the word is primary for Luke.[35] The Hellenistic world identified certain persons (real or mythological) as saviors on the basis of the benefits that they brought: Caesar Augustus for peace, Asklepios for healing, Isis for mastery over the sea, and so on. These saviors were also called "benefactors" and their coming was described as "gospel," or good news. Danker notes that Jesus is called a benefactor in Acts 10:38, and the healing of a cripple in his name is described as a "benefit" in Acts 4:8 (though English translations do not always use these words). Thus, salvation for Luke can mean the bestowal of any divine gift. Healings, exorcisms, and miracles are all saving acts. The primary benefit that Jesus offers, however, is the forgiveness of sins, which assures the individual of a renewed relationship with God.

Charles Talbert assumes a similar view of salvation when he likens Jesus in Luke-Acts to the "immortals" of Greek mythology.[36] Immortals were persons like Hercules or Dionysus who were originally mortal beings but who underwent a transformation and became gods. This transformation was frequently expressed in terms of a visible ascent into heaven. After the immortals were deified, they could intervene on behalf of their favorites. Acts, then, might be taken as presenting the salvation that Jesus offers from heaven as analogous to the help that Greek persons were accustomed to expecting from ascended and deified figures of mythology.

Gerhard Voss argues that Luke understands salvation in the Old Testament sense, as protection and liberation from the interference of foreign powers.[37] Healings and exorcisms are saving acts because they remove chosen people, from the sphere of Satan's power. Forgiveness of sins likewise brings liberation from bondage, that is from the servitude that people enter when they turn away from God.

Paul Minear follows this same line of thinking in his book *To Heal and to Reveal*, where he interprets Luke's presentation of Jesus as a prophet.[38] Specifically, Acts identifies Jesus as "the prophet like Moses" promised in Deuteronomy 18:15–16 (Acts 3:22; cf. 7:37). Acceptance of this prophet brings forgiveness of sins and times of refreshing from the Lord (Acts 3:19–20), but rejection of this prophet brings destruction (Acts 3:23). Elsewhere in Acts, it is said that Moses was rejected because people did not understand that through him God was giving them salvation (7:25). In Luke's gospel, Jesus' life is described in terms that recall elements of the Moses story and, at one point, the work that Jesus must accomplish is even described as an "exodus" (9:31). Accordingly, Minear decides that Luke understands Jesus as one who, like Moses, has established a new covenantal basis for God's people and inaugurated a new epoch. Once more, God has heard cries for deliverance and, through Jesus, has redeemed captives from their slavery.

These models for understanding Luke's portrait of Jesus have implications that go beyond soteriology but, as we have indicated here, they do favor particular interpretations of Luke's concept of salvation. One of the most in-depth studies of salvation in Luke's writings, however, is a book by I. Howard Marshall entitled *Luke: Historian and Theologian*.[39] Marshall believes that salvation is the principal theme of both Luke and Acts.

Marshall emphasizes that, for Luke, salvation is "of God" (Acts 28:28). God is the true savior (Luke 1:47). Salvation is the gift of God, allotted to those whom God calls or chooses (Acts 2:39; 11:18). This view derives from the Old Testament, where God saves people by divine prerogative. God may simply choose to forgive sins and remember them no more (Jer 31:34).

The central point of the book of Acts, Marshall contends, is that this divine prerogative has now been transferred to Jesus. The resurrection and the exaltation of Jesus signify that God has made Jesus Lord (Acts 2:36), and "whoever calls upon the name of the Lord will be saved" (Acts 2:21). As Lord, Jesus has been given the right to forgive sins and to bestow salvation.

The interesting thing about this understanding of salvation is that it does not make much of the death of Jesus. Although Acts occasionally refers to Jesus' death on the cross as having some salvific value (20:28), the speeches in Acts usually mention Jesus' death only as a prelude to announcing the resurrection (e.g., 2:23–24; 3:13–15; 4:10). In proclaiming the "message of salvation" (13:26), it is the exaltation of Jesus by God that counts. In short, Marshall believes Acts presents Jesus as providing salvation, not primarily by virtue of his suffering and death, but by virtue of his resurrection, exaltation and continuing lordship.[40]

As for the nature of this salvation, Marshall reads Acts as emphasizing present benefits over future ones. It is true that salvation includes eternal life (13:48) and deliverance from the final judgment (2:19–21), but in general Luke stresses two aspects of salvation that Jesus provides right now: forgiveness of sins and the gift of the Holy Spirit (2:11).

How are these received? Marshall notes a strong emphasis on conversion in the book of Acts.[41] The first step in conversion seems always to be the preaching of the word about Jesus. Those who hear this word must accept it with repentance and faith. Repentance in Acts signifies turning toward God, an inward change of heart that finds expression in outward actions (26:20). Faith may mean either belief in the message about Jesus (8:12) or belief in Jesus himself (16:31).

Marshall notes that this emphasis on acceptance of the word brings Luke close to embracing a doctrine of salvation by works. But Luke ultimately avoids this by insisting that God, who sends out the word, also prepares the hearts of men and women to receive it. Peter can exhort people to "save themselves" (2:40) but, in reality, it is by God's grace that people come to faith (18:27). The proclaimed word is the gospel of the grace of God (20:24). Luke does emphasize piety and obedience to God's law, but salvation is through "the grace of the Lord Jesus" (15:11).

The Holy Spirit

The Holy Spirit, of course, figures greatly in the book of Acts—so much so that Luke's second volume has been referred to as "the gospel of the Holy Spirit."[42] Scholars attempt to discern how Luke's view of the Holy Spirit fits in with his overall theology.

Some scholars relate Luke's interest in the Holy Spirit to his view of salvation history. Even before Hans Conzelmann advanced the idea that Luke divides history into three epochs (Israel, Jesus, the church), Heinrich von Baer discerned three phrases for the activity of the Holy Spirit in Luke's writings.[43] Luke, he suggested, thinks of the Old Testament period as a time when the Holy Spirit was promised, the life of Jesus as a time when the Holy Spirit intervened through select individuals, and his own day as a time when the Holy Spirit directs the missionary activity of the entire church.

Others prefer to relate Luke's view of the Spirit to a twofold scheme of promise and fulfillment.[44] In Acts, the Holy Spirit is referred to as "the promise of the Father" (1:4). The outpouring of the Spirit at Pentecost also fulfills promises of Old Testament prophets (2:16), as well as promises made by John the Baptist (Luke 3:16; Acts 1:5) and by Jesus (Acts 1:8).

At issue in these discussions is the degree of continuity that Luke presumes to exist between his own time and the past. Some scholars believe that Luke intends for the outpouring of the Spirit at Pentecost to mark the beginning of a new covenant that supersedes the old covenant of the law.[45] This view is bolstered by evidence that the Pentecost festival itself was an occasion for the Jews to celebrate the giving of the law at Sinai. Thus, the story in Acts 2 is understood as contrasting the greater gift of the Spirit with the former gift of the law. It is not certain, however, that the Pentecost festival was associated with the Sinai covenant at the time when Acts was written.[46]

Jacob Jervell does not believe Luke distinguishes greatly between the Spirit's role in the past and in his own present.[47] Luke does not regard the Spirit as merely promised during the Old Testament period, but as active through the prophets (Acts 1:16; 4:25; 28:25). In Acts, the Spirit remains primarily the Spirit of prophecy, testifying that the Messiah promised by the prophets of old has come.

Still, Luke is regarded by most scholars as presenting the relationship of the Spirit to humankind as changed after Pentecost. As one writer puts it, after Pentecost the Spirit's activity in human life is "*inward* where before it had been outward, *permanent* where before it had been spasmodic, *corporate* where before it had been individual, and *universal* where before it had been national" (i.e., exclusive to the Jews). Moreover, the Spirit is "now known to be the Spirit *of Christ* and so has a personal character and quality which before could not have been clearly perceived."[48]

1. *Who or what is the Holy Spirit?* The same question arises with Luke's concept of the Holy Spirit as with his concept of salvation: is the background for his understanding to be found in Greek or Hebrew thinking? At the risk of oversimplifying, it may be said that the Greek view considers the Spirit more as a force within people while the Old Testament portrays the Spirit as an independent entity that operates outside of people.[49]

Eduard Schweizer notes that Luke generally avoids representation of the Spirit in the animistic sense of the Old Testament, as an independent power that leaps on persons for a time and then abandons them later.[50] In Acts, the Spirit is described as a fluid: people are said to be "full of the Spirit" (6:3; 7:55; 11:24). Schweizer admits, however, that Luke sometimes does retain the Old Testament sense in order to emphasize that the Spirit is fundamentally the Spirit of God. Believers have the Spirit as a permanent possession but not as a natural one. Luke wants to emphasize the lasting union with the Spirit enjoyed by believers but he also wants to present every actualization of the Spirit as an act of God.

Roger Stronstad thinks that Luke's concept of the Spirit draws heavily from the Old Testament background.[51] In his work *The Charismatic Theology of St. Luke*, he notes a preference for septuagintal terminology in Luke's descriptions of the Spirit and also singles out three parallel motifs: 1) Just as in the Old Testament the Spirit is transferred from one leader to another (e.g., Moses to Joshua, Elijah to Elisha), so also in Acts the Spirit is transferred from Jesus to his disciples; 2) Just as in the Old Testament the gift of the Spirit is often accompanied by signs that confirm God's call to leadership (e.g., prophesying), so also in Acts the gift of the Spirit is attested to by observable signs, such as speaking with other tongues and prophesying (19:6); 3) Just as in the Old Testament the gift of the Spirit endows people with skills appropriate to fulfill the call of God (e.g., perception, wisdom, knowledge, military prowess), so also in Acts the Holy Spirit enables the church for its mission to witness (1:8). Stronstad also notes, however, that Luke's concept of the Holy Spirit differs from that of the Old Testament in that the gift is no longer restricted to chosen leaders but is potentially universal.

The conclusion, then, of both these scholars is that Luke's concept of the Spirit transcends Greek and Old Testament thought, while incorporating elements of both. Sometimes it is said that Luke thinks of the Holy Spirit as a "person," a concept distinct from either the Old Testament idea of an animistic force or the Greek image of a fluid. The Spirit speaks (10:19) and calls persons to ministry (13:2). People lie to the Spirit (5:3) and put the Spirit to the test (5:9). Thus, Francois Bovon says that the Holy Spirit gains a personal stature for Luke, comparable to that of God or Christ.[52] John Hull observes, "If there is no doctrine of the Trinity as such in Acts, all the materials are certainly there."[53]

A few scholars have sounded words of caution on this point. G. W. H. Lampe wonders whether the personal characteristics that appear to be attributed to the Holy Spirit in Luke's writings should not be properly referred to God.[54] The Spirit itself is but a mode of God's activity, the power through which God deals with people. F. F. Bruce notes that some of these personal qualities attributed to the Spirit derive from a close identification of the Spirit with the apostolic community.[55] It is when Ananias and Sapphira attempt to deceive this community that Peter accuses them of lying to the Spirit and putting the Spirit to the test (4:32—5:11). Similarly, in Acts 15 the community issues a decree that reads, "It seemed good to the Holy Spirit and to us . . ." (15:28). What we have in Acts, then, is a tendency to credit the Spirit with personal movements of either God or the church. Whether this is just a manner of speaking on Luke's part or whether Luke really conceives of the Spirit as a divine person remains open to debate.

2. *What does the Spirit do?* In some ways, the role Luke attributes to the Spirit in Acts is fairly limited. The Spirit is not explicitly described as generating faith, as bringing people to salvation, or as providing any guarantee of salvation. No one is ever "washed in the Spirit" (cf. 1 Cor 6:11) or "sealed with the Spirit" (Eph 4:30). Neither is the Spirit linked to the moral life of believers. We find no reference here to the "fruit of the Spirit" mentioned by Paul (Gal 4:22–23) or to any work of inward purification that the Spirit might be expected to accomplish. Luke ignores or neglects these aspects of the Spirit's work in order to concentrate on the one function he considers indispensable: providing Jesus' disciples with power to be witnesses (1:8).[56] As such, Luke's understanding of the Spirit (and for that matter, his understanding of the church) is expressed largely in terms of mission.[57]

Leo O'Reilly describes the Holy Spirit in Acts as "the source of word and sign."[58] By this he means that the Spirit gives the apostles power to preach and also to perform miracles. The word of God preached by Jesus' disciples comes into being on Pentecost by the power of the Spirit. Peter's sermon on that occasion and other proclamations of the word in Acts show continuity with the prophets of the past, for Luke regards preaching of the word as a prophetic activity empowered by the Spirit. Both prophetic speech and the preaching of the word are closely linked with the gift of the Holy Spirit in Acts (2:17–20; 4:31).

The working of miracles is more often linked with the name of Jesus.[59] Still, O'Reilly considers miracles a part of Spirit-empowered witness because they are termed "signs and wonders" and frequently accompany the preaching of the word. The miracles authenticate the word, attest to its divine origin, and make it possible for the disciples to speak more boldly. In addition, the miracles themselves are interpreted as signs of the glory that Jesus has received from God and so they too are proclamations that Jesus is Lord (Acts 3:1—4:12).

In short, the Spirit's role in Acts is to empower the disciples in their prophetic proclamation of word and sign. This proclamation announces and manifests the salvation offered by Christ. Together, word and sign constitute a potent reality capable of effecting the very salvation that they proclaim.

Jacob Jervell offers a similar analysis: The Spirit in Acts is the Spirit of prophecy.[60] The Spirit is primarily responsible for the manner of speaking (with boldness and accompanied by miracles) rather than for the content of the proclamation. The content, according to Luke, is wholly derived from scripture (Acts 17:11). Of course, what is in the scriptures was given by the Spirit too (Acts 1:16; 4:25; 7:51–52; 28:25), but Luke does not envision the Spirit now as adding anything new to the word of God already written down. When the Spirit does speak, the words are of a different kind: directions for the life of the church and the conduct of its mission (8:29; 10:19; 11:28; 13:2; 15:28; 20:23; 21:4; 21:11). In no case are the contemporary words of the Spirit ever called the word of God or the gospel. Only the words of the Spirit in scripture are authoritative—Paul chooses not to obey advice offered "through the Spirit" in one church (Acts 21:4).[61]

The point Jervell wishes to make is that the Spirit in Acts is primarily responsible for confirming and supporting prophecy already given in scripture. The boldness of the apostles' preaching and the miracles that accompany it demonstrate that their proclamation is the word of God. Thus, the Spirit secures the identity of the church as the people of God who are in continuity with scripture.

O'Reilly and Jervell agree, then, that the Spirit in Acts is immediately responsible for empowering Jesus' disciples to preach and to work miracles. Both scholars, however, envision this somewhat limited role as serving a larger purpose. For O'Reilly, the Spirit is ultimately responsible for bringing people to salvation because this is the effect of the word and sign proclamation that the Spirit produces. For Jervell, the Spirit is responsible for establishing the church as the people of God because the boldness and the miracles given by the Spirit demonstrate a continuity with the prophecies of scripture.

3. *How is the Spirit received?* At the conclusion of his sermon

on the day of Pentecost, Peter tells the crowd that has gathered, "Repent and be baptized every one of you in the name of Jesus Christ . . . and you will receive the gift of the Holy Spirit" (Acts 2:38). At first, this may appear to offer a divine order for the life of faith: 1) repentance, 2) baptism, 3) gift of the Spirit. But, actually, the situation is more complex. As F. F. Bruce notes,[62] the Spirit may also come after baptism and the laying on of hands (with some lapse of time between these two); after baptism accompanied immediately by the laying on of hands; or before baptism as the divine response to inward faith (Acts 8:14–17; 19:1–7; 10:44–48).

Some scholars argue that the pattern expressed in Acts 2:38 is what Luke considers normative, while the other accounts record exceptional cases.[63] Acts 8:14–17 relates the first time the Spirit is given to Samaritans and Acts 10:44–48, the first time the Spirit is given to Gentiles. Acts 19:1–7 records an unusual encounter with former disciples of John the Baptist. In any case, these exceptional accounts testify to Luke's conviction that, even though the chronology may vary, repentance, baptism, and the gift of the Spirit are three things that go together. Michael Quesnel reasons that the lack of uniformity derives from a wide diversity of church practice based on varying milieu.[64] The procedure for integrating new believers into the community varies in different cultures and the Holy Spirit is not expected to always manifest itself in the same way.

Other elements are sometimes stressed. Lampe emphasizes prayer.[65] In Luke's gospel, Jesus promises that God will give the Holy Spirit to those who ask (11:13). Jesus himself receives the Spirit while praying (Luke 3:21–22) and in Acts the apostles await the Spirit in prayer (1:14). Again, in Acts 4:31 disciples are filled with the Holy Spirit in response to prayer. Peter and John pray that the Holy Spirit might come upon the Samaritan believers before laying hands on them (8:15, 17).

The laying on of hands itself is of interest to Ernst Käsemann.[66] By stressing this rite in certain places (Acts 8:17; 19:6; cf. 9:17; 13:3), Luke wishes to centralize apostolic authority. Philip cannot impart the Spirit to the Samaritans, according to Käsemann, because he has not been commissioned to do so. The necessary laying on of hands must be performed by representatives of the apostolic community in Jerusalem. Similarly, believers in Ephe-

sus who were once disciples of John the Baptist do not even know
that there is a Holy Spirit until Paul comes to lay hands on them.
Paul himself received the Spirit in the same way from Ananias.
Thus Luke favors a dogmatic theory of succession, by which the
Spirit is only imparted through the ministry of the one legitimate
church. Käsemann himself objects strongly to this idea, which he
regards as nonhistorical and as representative of what he calls
"early catholicism." Similarly, Francois Bovon notes that in Acts
the Spirit sometimes seems "dangerously at the disposition of the
apostles."[67]

C. K. Barrett, however, reaches the opposite conclusion.[68]
Luke believes the church is the institutional home of the Holy
Spirit but, at the same time, the church is transcended and con-
trolled by the Spirit. A primary point in the story of the Samaritans
is that Simon the magician is unable to acquire the power to pass
on the Spirit no matter how much he is willing to pay. The Spirit in
Acts is always *given*. This gift of the Spirit is something on which
the church can depend but it is not something the church can
control. Likewise, James Dunn does not regard any of the reports
of people receiving the Spirit in Acts as paradigmatic: God gives
the Holy Spirit directly to faith.[69]

Finally, we recall the observation of I. H. Marshall that the
gift of the Spirit is one aspect of the salvation that Luke links
ultimately to Jesus' exaltation as Lord (see above, p. 49).[70] From
this perspective, the Spirit is given by Jesus according to his own
sovereign prerogative. Stories in Acts indicate a tendency for Jesus
to give the Spirit to people who repent, pray, have faith, are baptized, and so on. But in the final analysis, Jesus can and does give
the Spirit to whomever he chooses.

Observations and Conclusions

Beverly Gaventa notes that in current scholarship there are at
least four methods employed for identifying the theology of Acts.[71]
The first focuses on discernment of editorial changes that Luke is
believed to have made in his sources. A second focuses on the
speeches of Acts, under the assumption that these are composed
by Luke and provide the most direct access to his thinking. A third

identifies "key texts" as especially significant—the ascension narrative, for instance, or the story of Pentecost. A fourth emphasizes particular themes, such as salvation history or promise and fulfillment, which scholars believe are developed throughout the book.

All of these methods are problematic insofar as they neglect certain aspects of Acts while accenting others.[72] But there is also an increasing tendency for scholars to use such methods eclectically or, at least, to compare their conclusions with those reached by another route. This, in fact, is what we have done in this chapter.

The book of Acts is *theocentric*. God is presented as the director of history, and the hope of humanity is presented as dependent on God's promises. Acts is also *christocentric*, for God exalts Jesus to become "Lord of all" (2:36; 10:36). Finally, Acts is *pneumocentric* (spirit-centered) for the exalted Lord Jesus pours out the Holy Spirit on his followers so that they might become his witnesses.

We have found evidence for both salvation-history and promise-fulfillment motifs in Acts. We have also seen signs that Luke draws from a wide variety of backgrounds, embracing now the Hebrew ideology of the Old Testament, now the Hellenistic philosophy of the Greek world.

There is one point on which all the scholars discussed in this chapter would agree: Luke is a theologian. He wrote the book of Acts, not simply to tell interesting stories or to record facts for posterity, but in order to put forth his own distinctive ideas about God's interaction with us through Jesus Christ and the Holy Spirit.

4
The Church in Acts:
Eschatology and Ecclesiology

The book of Acts tells the story of the early church. The outpouring of the Spirit on Pentecost in chapter 2 is often viewed as the "birthday of the church," and the remainder of the narrative may be read as an account of the church at work. The extent to which Acts can be read as a *history* of the church will be considered in the next chapter. Here, we will consider Luke's theology of the church, his beliefs about the nature and the mission of the church as they appear in his writings.

Lukan Eschatology

Opinions regarding Luke's ecclesiology are usually dependent on opinions regarding his eschatology—that is, his beliefs about "last things," such as the parousia and the kingdom of God. Different views on Lukan eschatology lead to different conceptions of the church.[1]

1. *Delayed eschatology.* Hans Conzelmann's proposal is that Luke believes the parousia has been indefinitely postponed.[2] Whereas the first Christians believed Jesus would return soon, Luke realizes that this has not happened and possibly will not happen for quite some time. Evidence that Luke believes this is adduced mainly from his editing of Mark's gospel.[3] For example, where Jesus in Mark promises that his disciples will not die before they "see that the kingdom of God has come with power" (Mark 9:1), in Luke, Jesus says only that they will not die before they "see

the kingdom," that is, see what it is like (Luke 9:27). Or again, Luke appends to Mark's parable about servants who must be ready for their master's return (Mark 13:33–37), explicit advice regarding how those servants must act if their master is delayed (Luke 12:35–48).

Conzelmann believes this view of delayed eschatology led Luke to develop a concept of salvation history, whereby Jesus was believed to have come in the "middle of time" rather than at the end of time. The implications for ecclesiology are profound. Luke perceives an "Age of the Church" on this side of the life of Jesus comparable to the "Age of Israel" on the other side of the life of Jesus. The church is not a spontaneous body soon to be taken out of this world, but a preordained institution that has a purpose within world history. Its primary function is to mediate the saving effects of redemptive history and it does this by preserving and proclaiming tradition. In a sense, salvation is something that happened in the past (during the life of Jesus) and something that will happen again in the future (when Jesus returns). The church links believers to these events by keeping alive recollections of the past and promises for the future.

Other scholars who think Acts is written from the perspective of delayed eschatology include Ernst Käsemann and Ernst Haenchen, whose views on various matters regarding the church will be discussed below.[4]

2. *Imminent eschatology*. A. J. Mattill argues that Luke does not present the parousia as postponed but as imminent.[5] Indeed, Peter announces at Pentecost that the "last days" have arrived (Acts 2:17). The heart of Mattill's exegesis focuses on verses containing the Greek word *mellō*, which he says should be translated "about to." Thus, Acts 17:31 does not merely say that the world *will be* judged but that the world is *about to* be judged (see also 24:15, 25). Two other scholars, Robert Smith and Richard Hiers, hold that Luke manages to simultaneously explain the delay that has occurred and encourage new hope for an imminent end.[6] The end could not come until the apostles had carried out their mission of taking the gospel to the ends of the earth, but insofar as this mission is fulfilled in Acts, it is *now* proper to expect the end at any time. John T. Carroll in *Response to the End of History* calls atten-

tion to the signs by which Luke's community is advised to recognize that the end is near.[7] While granting that some delay has already occurred, Luke wants his readers to keep alert: the return of Jesus will be sudden and soon but believers informed by Jesus' teaching (Luke 21:25–32) and by scripture (Acts 2:17–21) need not be caught off guard.

The view of an imminent eschatology leads to perceptions concerning the role of the church in Acts different from those consistent with the view of delayed eschatology. Mattill actually believes the church has a role in effecting the end. Luke urges an early completion of the mission to the nations in order to bring about the day of the Lord "ahead of schedule." Carroll also thinks imminent eschatology emphasizes urgency in mission, though he interprets this as simply commending fervency to those who might otherwise become complacent. Belief in an imminent end counters "business as usual" orientations that fail to reckon with Jesus' return.

3. *Present eschatology*. Helmut Flender believes that the ascension rather than the parousia is the significant eschatological event for Luke.[8] Since the ascension has already taken place, the hope of eschatological salvation, far from being directed toward an indefinite future, is represented as fulfilled. Flender notes that Luke transfers to the ascension benefits that are usually associated with the parousia, including the outpouring of the Spirit. Likewise, Eric Franklin believes Luke solves the problem of the nonoccurrence of the parousia not by justifying the delay but by trivializing it.[9] Since the hopes of Israel are already realized in the exaltation of Christ, it makes little difference when the final parousia will come. Robert Maddox also thinks that Acts depicts the kingdom of God as a present reality, a joyful and confident time in which the essential expectations of the end-time have already been realized.[10] J. Bradley Chance believes that, in Luke-Acts, Jesus inaugurates the New Age in its fullest eschatological sense, such that the time of the church described in Acts coincides with the messianic reign of Christ.[11]

This understanding of eschatology generally does not lead scholars to view Acts according to eras of salvation history like those proposed by Conzelmann, but according to models of promise and fulfillment. Rather than situating the church in an historical waiting period, these models understand the church as situated at the glorious consummation of the ages. How long these "last days" will last is irrelevant. The present role of the church is not so much persistence or preservation as it is appropriation of the promises of God.

4. *Future eschatology*. Hans Bartsch believes Luke's gospel was written to warn against the very views that Flender thinks it espouses.[12] Luke wants to arouse hope for the end-time on the part of Christians who are content with the experience of salvation to be found in this world. Against those who are interpreting Jesus' resurrection and exaltation as the final consummation of salvation, Luke encourages watching for what is still to come (Luke 21:36). The timing of the event is less important than its certainty. This view is similar to that espoused by Charles Talbert, who thinks Luke-Acts counters Gnostic identifications of either Jesus' ascension or Pentecost with the inauguration of the kingdom of God.[13] Luke emphasizes the parousia as an observable, historical (though still future) event.

Beverly Gaventa, who also argues for future eschatology in Luke-Acts, does so with reference to promise/fulfillment motifs.[14] Acts narrates the fulfillment of numerous promises, including the gift of the Spirit and the accomplishment of the worldwide mission (1:8). Thus Luke's reader is assured that the promises of eschatological salvation linked to the parousia, though still future, will be fulfilled as well.

Again, perceptions of the role of the church based on a future-oriented eschatology differ from those perceptions based on a present-oriented view. The church's primary task, according to this view, must be to prepare people for the coming judgment, to proclaim the relative transiency of this world, and to maintain hope in the ultimate salvation that awaits the faithful.

5. *Mixed views*. Some scholars say that Luke appears to argue for both delayed and imminent eschatology because he is combatting errors that result when either view is taken to an extreme.[15] He wants to caution those who are waiting for the end to come at any moment that there might be a delay and remind them that the church has a mission to perform in the meantime. But he also

wants to encourage those who have lost hope or become lax by insisting that the end *could* come at any time.

E. Earle Ellis tries to harmonize the present and future eschatology themes in Acts.[16] He advocates a two-stage eschatology for Luke, by which eschatological hopes find initial fulfillment in the exaltation of Jesus but still await final consummation at a future parousia. The kingdom of God has both a present and a future dimension. The church partakes of the present dimension now but also proclaims an even greater experience of salvation that is still to come.

Church Leadership in Acts

Questions about church leadership in Acts usually begin with the apostles. As early as 1936, B. S. Easton published a work that articulated many of the issues in the current debate.[17] His thesis: Luke describes the polity of the early church as dominated by a Christian Sanhedrin in Jerusalem. The college of the apostles there has governing authority over all of the communities founded by missionaries. In particular, Paul is presented as subordinate to the apostles. Paul repeatedly travels to Jerusalem, where his ministry receives confirmation or approval from the leadership there (9:26; 11:30; 12:25; 15:2, 6, 25; 18:22; 21:15). His preaching of the resurrection rests on Christ's appearances to the apostles rather than on his own experience on the Damascus road (13:30–31).

Günter Klein takes this argument a step further.[18] In his study, *Die Zwölf Apostel*, he alleges that Luke invented the concept of the twelve apostles in an effort to centralize authority in the developing church. Walter Schmithals thinks Klein really means to say (or should have said) that Luke was the first to restrict the apostolate to the twelve in Jerusalem[19] (Mark 6:30 and Matthew 10:2 also identify disciples of Jesus as apostles). In any case, Luke uses the term "apostles" for Jesus' disciples five times in his gospel and twenty-six times in Acts. The two references to Paul and Barnabas as "apostles" in Acts 14:4, 14 are assumed to derive from one of Luke's sources and to represent a popular sense of the word meaning simply "messenger." In Acts 1:21–25, qualifications for apostleship are defined in terms that Paul and

Barnabas would not meet. Klein and Schmithals agree that Luke emphasizes the authority of the twelve as apostles in contradistinction to Paul and other missionaries.

Klein sees in Acts the development of a doctrine of apostolic succession. The seven deacons chosen in Acts 6:3 are ordained by the apostles (6:6), and in 14:23 elders are appointed by Paul and Barnabas, who are under the apostles' authority. We have already seen, in chapter 3, that Ernst Käsemann interprets the "laying on of hands" in Acts as a sign of apostolic control over the transference of spiritual power and authority (see above, pp. 55–56). Both Klein and Käsemann read Acts as establishing an "early catholic" ecclesiastical system with Jerusalem as the apostolic seat. Both, we might add, regard this development negatively, as a falling away from the truth and freedom of the gospel. To these studies might be compared a work of Cardinal Jean Danielou that affirms the hierarchical and institutional character of the twelve in Acts as historical, and likewise attributes the tendency toward limited apostolic succession to genuine tradition rather than to Lukan redaction.[20]

Recent scholars have tended to deny the presence of "early catholicism" in Acts.[21] Conzelmann and Schmithals think the importance of the apostles as legitimators of the tradition is emphasized, but see no evidence for apostolic succession.[22] The laying on of hands may simply confer a blessing, without implying any difference in rank between those who give or receive the blessing (cf. 13:3). Eduard Schweizer believes that leadership in Acts seems to arise as needed: the basis is functional and charismatic, not prescribed.[23] Kevin Giles notes that, in Luke's gospel, the disciples who become apostles in Acts are told that leadership does not place them at the top of a spiritual hierarchy; rather, the leader is one who serves (Luke 22:26).[24] This "spiritual egalitarianism" taught by Jesus in the gospel prevails throughout the church in Acts: the Spirit is given to all (2:38–39) and many significant advances are made by ordinary believers (e.g., 11:19). Although Luke mentions "apostles," "deacons," "elders," and "prophets," his favorite word for the community is simply "the brethren" (over twenty-five times), a term that relativizes the significance of ecclesiastical offices.[25]

W. Ward Gasque gives an historical perspective to this debate.[26] "Gone are the days," he writes, "when theologians used to
find *the* biblical church order in Acts, be it presbyterial, congregational, or episcopal." Scholars who took such an approach, Gasque
observes, usually found what they were looking for because Acts
displays a variety of leadership forms. Rather than presenting any
one polity as dominant, Acts affirms "unity in diversity."[27]

Joseph Tyson considers the question of authority in the early
church from the perspective of a sequential reading of the entire
narrative.[28] In the first part of the book he recognizes that the
apostles do exercise practical (4:34–35), spiritual (2:42–43) and
sometimes fearful (5:1–11) authority. But after chapter 12, the
leadership in Jerusalem moves toward nonapostolic figures, such
as James and the elders (cf. 15:6, 22; 21:18). Once the narrative
shifts to accounts of Paul's missionary work, the authorities in
Jerusalem no longer figure greatly. The practice of evangelizing
churches and then returning to them suggests that the evangelists
themselves exercise authority in these communities. The references to Paul and Barnabas as apostles in 14:4, 14 may provide
subtle indication that their authority among the Gentiles was analogous to that of the twelve among the Jews. In short, Luke is concerned not only with continuity in his depiction of church leadership, but also with change. He is sensitive to historical development and does not want the structures of one place or time to be
imposed upon another.

Tyson's last comment touches on another problem that is
often raised in contemporary evaluations of Lukan ecclesiology:
the structures of church leadership described in Acts are undeni-
ably patriarchal, that is, male-dominated. Some scholars, such as
Elisabeth Fiorenza and Elisabeth Tetlow suspect Luke of under-
playing the roles of women in his account due to his own sexist
bias.[29] Others believe the patriarchal nature of the early church in
Acts simply reflects the historical realities of the period—in fact,
Luke is said to go out of his way to call attention to the roles
women were able to play (Acts 1:14; 2:17–18; 12:2; 16:13–15;
18:18, 26), roles admittedly limited by the conventions of society
at the time.

Growth and Triumph

The story of the church in Acts is a story marked by growth and triumph. The ongoing success of the church's mission is stressed in a number of summaries that mark its progress: 1:14; 2:41; 4:4; 5:14; 6:7; 9:31; 11:21, 24; 12:24; 14:1; 16:5; 19:20; 28:30–31. Indeed, Ernst Haenchen thinks the real subject of Acts is the word of God and its growth, proclaimed by people and authenticated by God through signs and miracles.[30]

Three of the passages mentioned above refer specifically to the growth of the *word* (6:7; 12:24; 19:20), in what appear to be descriptions of the growth of the *church*. Jerome Kodell takes these as allusions to the parable of the sower in Luke's gospel (8:4–15), where the seed represents the word of God.[31] The numerical increase in the church is evidence that the seed has fallen on good soil and is bearing much fruit. Luke sees the word of God as so embedded in Christian community that he can say "the word of God grew" when the church adds new members.

Schuyler Brown calls attention to the fact that the church grows in spite of persecution, or even because of it (8:1–4).[32] Suffering is a cause for joy (5:41; 9:16; 15:26; 21:13) because it serves as a catalyst for intensified missionary activity. This theme of the successful perseverance of the church in the face of many tribulations is important for Luke, Brown surmises, because it serves to establish the legitimacy of the tradition preserved in his writings. The apostles did not give in to apostasy but kept the true faith, which is now the faith of the church in which Christians stand. Christians in Luke's own day are presumed to remain faithful not by proving the strength of their individual faith but by remaining in *the* faith, that is, the historic faith preserved by the apostles.

Jacob Jervell thinks the miracles in Acts serve a legitimating function also.[33] The miracles that Paul works characterize him as an authorized preacher and missionary. Similarly, O'Reilly (see above, pp. 53–54) thinks that the miracles serve as signs in Acts to authenticate the word and enable the apostles to preach more boldly.[34] They also provoke faith and thus serve to promote the growth of the church. So, also, Paul Achtemeier: "It is rather clear

in Acts that the miracles were an effective device for turning people to faith" (cf. 9:35, 42; 13:12; 16:30, 33; 19:17).[35]

For G. W. H. Lampe, Luke's point of view concerning miracles is much closer to that of the Old Testament, where signs and
wonders are manifest operations of God by which judgment or
salvation is brought to people.[36] The miracles in Acts should not be
regarded as "conjuring tricks, designed to induce belief in God,"
but as "focal points at which the continuous activity of God becomes manifest both to his people and to their oppressors." The
miracles are visible evidence of the new age that brings fulfillment
of prophetic hopes.[37]

Susan Garrett interprets the miracles and triumphant victories
in Acts against the background of Hellenistic views concerning
magic and the demonic.[38] In her book, *The Demise of the Devil*,
she demonstrates that Acts presents Christian experience as a testimony to Christ's ultimate triumph over Satan. In Luke's day, Satan
was typically regarded as the ruler of this world. Luke's gospel
presents the ministry of Jesus as a struggle with this "strong one"
(11:21–22) that leads to the devil's downfall (10:17–18). The miracles performed by believers in Acts are a sign of Christian authority over the devil, authority that Jesus promised to his followers
(Luke 10:19). The resounding success of Christians at casting out
demons and healing the sick are especially telling signs of this
authority, for Satan is believed to be responsible for the activities
of demons and for disease. Acts also emphasizes the Christian
defeat of magicians and the winning away of their adherents (8:9–
13; 13:6–12; 19:11–20), for in Luke's world such magicians were
regarded as servants of Satan who derived their powers through
traffic with demons. Thus, Luke's word about the present authority of Christians over Satan was intended to be reassuring in a
world where the awful power of the devil was very real.

Luke's positive message is not itself evaluated positively by all
critics today. It is often said that he exhibits a "theology of glory"
that is out of touch with the harsh realities of life. In the real world,
Christians do not live as victoriously as they do in the book of Acts.
Foremost among such critics is Ernst Käsemann, who observes
that the motifs of growth and triumph that dominate this book do
so at the expense of any real theology of the cross.[39] The speeches

in Acts do not present the cross of Jesus as a scandal (cf. 1 Cor 1:23; Gal 5:11) but simply as a misunderstanding on the part of the Jews that Easter quickly corrects. It is because Luke does not understand the true meaning of the cross, Käsemann avers, that he is able to present the destiny of the church in terms of victory and success rather than in terms of suffering and rejection.

Three objections are raised against Käsemann's contention that in Luke-Acts a *theologia gloriae* replaces a *theologia crucis*. First, scholars such as Ulrich Wilckens and Joseph Fitzmyer have pointed out that this reading of Luke's theology can only be arrived at by way of comparison with Mark or with Paul.[40] Luke's theology should be interpreted on its own terms rather than evaluated according to whether it fits categories derived elsewhere. Second, C. K. Barrett and Beverly Gaventa have both indicated that the narrative of Acts presents a theology of the cross in a way that explicit discourse material does not.[41] Although the apostles do not talk greatly about the cross, they travel the way of the cross, enduring continued persecutions. Finally, Robert Tannehill notes that, despite the great success the gospel enjoys among Gentiles in Acts, it is repeatedly rejected by Jews (see below, pp. 104–05).[42] The book does not only tell a story of success, but also one of tragic failure.

Ministry to the Gentiles

The Gentile mission is a major concern for the church in the book of Acts. Jacques Dupont thinks Luke's interest in the Gentile mission is the reason for the book's existence.[43] The passage of Christianity from the Jewish world to the Gentile world is more significant than mere geographical or numerical expansion. In Luke's view, the salvation of God as revealed through messianic prophecies of the Old Testament (e.g., Isaiah 40:5; 49:6; cf. Luke 3:5; Acts 13:47) would be incomplete until the gospel had been taken decisively to the nations.

Stephen Wilson finds several motifs in Acts that explain how and why the Gentile mission comes about[44]: 1) the mission is no illegitimate offshoot of renegade Christians, but begins from Jerusalem (1:8) and is closely linked to the apostles (chapters 10—11, 15); 2) the extension of the church's mission to Gentiles takes place under the guidance and prompting of the Holy Spirit (10:44; 11:15; 15:8) and is accompanied by miraculous signs that indicate it is the work of God (10:46; 15:12); 3) the Gentile mission is not some "bright idea of the early church" but has its origin in the words and actions of Jesus (Luke 7:1–10; 24:47; Acts 1:8; 9:15; 22:21; 26:17); 4) the mission is foretold in scripture (Luke 3:6; Acts 2:17; 3:25; 13:47; 15:17), and 5) ministry to Gentiles finds theological justification in the notion that God is not partisan (Acts 14:15–17; 17:22–31). Wilson admits that these motifs are not necessarily consistent or even logical but represent a "jumble of miscellaneous themes, none of which is fully developed in itself or in relation to the others." The point, however, is that the fundamental motivation for the mission to the Gentiles was the prompting of God rather than simple Jewish rejection of the gospel.

The context in which Luke envisions the Gentile mission to take place is a matter of some controversy in Lukan studies. At least three different views are evident.

1. *Mission to Gentiles replaces mission to Israel.* Ernst Haenchen thinks that Luke has "written the Jews off."[45] The privileges of Israel are summarily dismissed by a revolutionary statement in Acts 10:35, that "in every nation, anyone who fears God and does what is right is acceptable to him." Three times in Acts, having met with rejection from Jews, Paul declares that he is turning to the Gentiles (13:44–46; 18:5–6; 28:23–28). The last of these, situated strategically at the end of the gospel, is especially relevant. The reader is left with the opinion that "the salvation of God has been sent to the Gentiles." The Jews rejected the message, but the Gentiles will listen.

This analysis represents a view that is widely accepted within Lukan studies. Such scholars as Augustin George, Joachim Gnilka, Robert Maddox, J. C. O'Neill, Jack Sanders, Joseph Tyson, and Stephen Wilson all agree that, for Luke, the mission to Israel is over.[46] Differences of opinion surface, however, regarding how this development is evaluated. Tyson thinks the failure of the Jewish mission is a matter of great sadness to Luke and constitutes a theological problem that he is not really able to explain. Maddox and Wilson both think the problem is only one of social identification, in that Luke's Gentile congregation must define their heritage over against Jewish opponents who claim that *they* are the true people of God.

Sanders has the most extreme view: Luke is basically anti-Semitic and regards the Jewish rejection of the gospel as typical for a people who have always rebelled against God (Acts 7:51–53).[47] Their exclusion from salvation is long overdue. In Luke's view, all Jews are, in principle, perverse; the world will be better off when they "get what they deserve and the world is rid of them." Sanders bases his controversial argument on certain blanket statements of condemnation scattered throughout Luke's writings (e.g., Luke 7:9; 11:29–32; Acts 2:23; 3:14–15; 4:10–12; 7:51–53; 13:46; 18:6; 28:25–28). In particular, the "whole house of Israel" is held responsible for the murder of Jesus (Acts 2:36; 3:14–15; 13:27). Even Christian Jews are portrayed as troublemakers (Acts 15:5). Sander's view agrees with the opinion of Luke-Acts advanced by Jewish scholar, Michael Cook.[48] Cook thinks that the repeated overtures to the Jews in Acts are only a device by which Luke hopes to assign responsibility for the underrepresentation of Jews in Christian ranks to Jewish intransigence. Luke thinks the transfer of salvation to the Gentiles is a judgment upon the Jews who receive only what retribution demands: the blood of the prophets will be required of them (Luke 11:50) and the stone which they have rejected will become that on which they are broken to pieces (Luke 20:17–18).

2. *Mission to Gentiles supplements mission to Israel.* An alternative proposal is that Luke envisions mission to Israel as continuing alongside the Gentile mission. The difficult passages for such a position are the three instances in which Paul responds to Jewish rejection by saying he will turn to the Gentiles (13:46; 18:6; 28:25–28). But these can be read as prophetic rebukes and not as final judgments—after Paul says this the first two times, he is found preaching to Jews again.

Robert Brawley notes several facets of Luke-Acts that indicate a conciliatory or apologetic tendency toward the Jews.[49] The rejection of Jesus and of Paul by certain Jews, he says, is presented in such a way that contemporary Jews will recognize Jesus and Paul as standing in line with the prophets (Luke 4:24). Furthermore, Luke describes large islands of acceptance: Jesus wins popular

support among the Jewish people, with the exception of those
crowds that are under the sway of the high priest. Paul is deemed
acceptable to the Pharisees (Acts 23:9). In fact Luke goes to great
lengths to present Paul as an exemplary Jew, born of the tribe of
Benjamin, trained as a Pharisee by Gamaliel, and zealous for the
traditions of the ancestors (Acts 22:3; 23:6). Even after he becomes a Christian, he remains a Jew—he promulgates the decree
regarding concessions Gentiles are to make when they join the
church (15:22) and he circumcises Timothy (16:3). This concern to
sketch Paul as a loyal Jew who does not teach apostasy from Judaism is intended, Brawley surmises, to conciliate Jewish objections
to Pauline Christianity. Thus, we may assume that Luke is still
interested in conversations with Israel. The success of the Gentile
mission has not supplanted hopes for reaching the Jews.

David Tiede and Robert Tannehill both regard closure of the
mission to Israel as impossible for Luke, on account of his aware-
ness of scriptural promises regarding Israel's salvation. Tiede notes
that Luke presents Jesus from the beginning as "one set for the fall
and rise of many in Israel" (Luke 2:34).[50] Acts narrates mostly the
fall, but ultimately Luke believes God's people will come around.
The turning to the Gentiles is presented in Deuteronomic and
prophetic terms as a reproach to Israel. At the end of the story,
God is contending with Israel, as God frequently does in the Old
Testament, but it would be unthinkable to imagine that God is
done with Israel or that eventual restoration and consolation could
not come. Tannehill thinks Acts ends tragically and that Luke has
no adequate explanation for why the plan of God for Israel has not
been fulfilled (see below, pp. 104–05). Still, Luke records amply
the promises that describe that plan (e.g., Luke 1:32–33, 76–79;
3:6) and so must believe it will eventually be fulfilled. Jesus is a
light not only for revelation to the Gentiles but also to God's
people Israel (Luke 2:32).

The view that Luke expects mission to Israel to continue is
also widely accepted in Lukan studies. Supporters include J. Bradley Chance, Eric Franklin, Donald Juel, and A. J. Mattill.[51]

3. *Mission to Gentiles completes mission to Israel*. Jacob Jervell
offers a third proposal.[52] Luke does not present the mission to
Israel as a failure, but as a great success. In spite of the numerous

accounts of rejection by small groups of Jews, Acts says that large numbers of Jews accept the gospel: three thousand in 2:41, five thousand in 4:4, and a great many more in 6:7. Finally it can be said that there are "myriads" of believers among the Jews, all zealous for the law (21:20). Thus, Jervell contends that Luke presents the mission to Israel as coming to an end at the conclusion of Acts because this phase of the mission is now complete. Israel has been successfully reached with the gospel; now it is time to take the gospel to the nations.

Of course, not all Jews have accepted God's word of salvation, but that, Luke believes, is precisely what the scriptures predict. The Jews who do believe represent the repentant remnant of Israel. The influx of Gentiles does not contradict this for Luke but confirms it, for he reads the scriptures as declaring that when Israel is restored even the Gentiles will repent. Thus, the Gentile mission is itself an outgrowth of Israel's faithfulness and obedience to God.

Jervell's view, though admittedly a minority position, has been influential in causing a number of scholars to rethink basic presuppositions about Luke-Acts. Joseph Fitzmyer, for instance, follows Jervell in asserting that there is no thought in Acts of promises to Israel being transferred to Gentile Christianity.[53] Rather, the Gentiles form part of the reconstituted Israel and inherit God's promises only by virtue of their new identity as part of this faithful remnant.

Jervell goes even further in one respect.[54] He believes that the only Gentiles who are saved in Acts are those who already have some connection with Israel—either proselytes (Gentile converts to Judaism) or "Godfearers" (Gentiles who attended synagogues although they had not actually converted or been circumcised). Large numbers of these Gentiles who were attracted to the Jewish religion were apparently to be found in the Roman world. Cornelius is certainly one of them: he is a devout man who fears God, gives alms, and prays constantly (Acts 10:2). The Gentiles addressed by Paul on his journeys are usually found attending the synagogue (e.g., 17:4) and are sometimes explicitly described as Godfearers (13:6, 26) or as worshipers of God (13:43; 16:14). By contrast, "pure Gentiles"—that is, pagans and idol worshipers—are rarely ever presented with the gospel and only scoff when they are (17:32). Dionysius the Areopagite (17:34) and the Philippian jailer (16:30–34) are the only possible exceptions to this, a meager haul at best. In short, Jervell contends that the church of Acts remains a church of Jews and semi-Jews. The so-called Gentile mission is but an extension or completion of the mission to Israel, analogous to missions already taking place within Judaism. The only Gentiles admitted to the church are those who would have been admitted to the synagogue.

This discussion concerns the issue on which there is wider divergence of opinion than any other in contemporary Lukan studies. This may be in part because, as Bovon observes, Acts seems paradoxically to be the book in the New Testament that is both the most universal in scope and the most favorable to Judaism.[55] Also, as Marilyn Salmon notes, the view as to whether Luke himself is Jewish or Gentile is quite significant, since this determines whether the polemical statements should be read as condemnations from without or as rebukes from within.[56] All of the scholars mentioned under the first proposal above think Luke is a Gentile, but Tiede and Jervell believe he and his congregation are probably Jewish.

Church and State

A tendency to stress compatibility between church and state is often noted in Acts. To begin with, Luke is said to present Christians as law-abiding citizens who pose no real threat to the social order. The public controversies that do occur are attributed to the work of other (usually Jewish) troublemakers. The proconsul at Corinth refuses to judge Paul because Jews do not accuse him of any real crime but are only upset over matters concerning their own law (18:14–15). In Ephesus, the town clerk makes it clear to the rioting crowd that *they* are the real lawbreakers (19:40). Later, Claudius Lysias, the centurion in charge of Paul's arrest, admits he is aware that Paul has done nothing guilty of death or imprisonment (23:29). The Roman rulers Festus (25:18–19) and King Agrippa (26:31–32) likewise testify to Paul's innocence. Hans Conzelmann summarizes Luke's position here as a "demonstration that Christian preaching does not impinge upon the power of the empire."[57] In short, Luke presents Christianity as a movement concerned with religious matters, not political ones. From a political standpoint, Christianity is irrelevant to the state.

By the same token, Luke is also said to portray the Roman Empire as a benevolent system that poses no threat to Christians. In numerous instances, Christians are rescued by Romans from possible harm at the hands of their enemies (18:12–16; 19:35–41; 23:10, 12–35). Paul takes pride in the fact that he is a Roman citizen (16:37–40; 22:25–29) and indeed his citizenship does seem to work to his advantage (23:27). Paul's appeal to Caesar (25:11–12) demonstrates his confidence in Roman justice. "Luke is not negative nor even neutral toward the empire," Paul Walaskay writes. "He has high regard for the imperial government and for those who administer it."[58] The theological foundation for such an idea, Walaskay believes, is the notion that there are two spheres—church and state—where power and authority are operative in the world. God ultimately stands behind both: God imparts to the emperor political authority that is analogous to the spiritual authority given to Jesus. "The state," Walaskay concludes, "is ordained by God to use its power for the benefit of all by obtaining peace and maintaining harmony among the diverse nations of the world."[59]

The data concerning the compatibility of church and state in Luke-Acts can be interpreted in different ways. Haenchen and others read Acts as presenting an apology to Rome on the part of the church (see above, pp. 15–16).[60] Walaskay thinks the apology is directed to the church on behalf of Rome: living peaceably with Rome is possible and advantageous.[61] Esler thinks the concern is to reassure Romans who have already become Christians that their faith will not conflict with their civil loyalties (see above, pp. 17–18).[62]

This theme has also been considered by Richard Cassidy in a way that contravenes all of the above interpretations.[63] In *Society and Politics in the Acts of the Apostles*, Cassidy finds the "compatibility" notion of church and state in Acts superficial. In fact, Luke presents Christians as boldly claiming that they must obey God, not human authorities (4:19–20; 5:29). In his trials, Paul makes it clear that he regards Jesus as his lord, not Caesar. The appeal to Caesar is done out of expedience not confidence—Paul fears Festus will hand him over to his enemies and so is "compelled" to appeal to Rome (25:9–11; 28:19). Luke does not portray political authorities as always just or fair. Herod and Pilate are named as conspirators in the plot to kill Jesus (4:27). Herod is responsible for killing the apostle James and unjustly imprisoning Peter (12:1–3). Lysias intends to torture Paul until he learns the latter is a Roman citizen (22:24–29). Felix keeps Paul in prison because he wants a bribe (24:26). In general, rulers seem more interested in what promotes their own interests than in justice (12:3; 24:27; 25:9).

The conclusion Cassidy draws is that Luke does not wish to foster idealistic notions about compatibility between church and state but wants to prepare Christians for identifying their allegiances and making an appropriate witness. He wants his readers to realize that, at times, disciples of Jesus may have to obey God over human leaders and suffer the consequences. As the narrative of Acts indicates, all sorts of outcomes are possible: sometimes God delivers the disciples, but at other times extended imprisonment or even death result. Given the uncertainty of world powers, it is possible that charges might be rejected or misinterpreted or simply delayed due to corruption and intrigue. The main point is that, whatever the experience and outcome, Christians are to remain faithful in their allegiance to God and steadfast in their witness to Jesus as Lord.

Congregational Life

Four aspects of congregational life in Luke-Acts have been dealt with in my book, *What Are They Saying About Luke?* (fellowship, worship and prayer, teaching, and mission).[64] We will deal with three more here.

1. *Baptism.* The paucity of literature dealing with the subject of baptism in Luke-Acts is surprising. Bovon, in his mammoth survey of scholarship, claims to be able to count on his fingers the studies devoted to Luke's concept of baptism.[65]

Kevin Giles notes that baptism appears to be nonsacramental in Acts.[66] It is never mentioned alone as a condition for being saved, but only in connection with something else, such as repentance (2:38) or calling on the Lord's name (22:16). Luke never depicts baptism as taking place in a cultic or liturgical setting (see

5:12, 36; 8:36–38; 10:44–48; 16:13–15, 33). Luke typically narrates baptism in the passive voice, so that it is impossible to tell exactly who does the baptizing (16:14–15, 30–34; 18:8; 19:1–7). Furthermore, Giles says, there is no suggestion that baptism incorporates a person into the community. I. H. Marshall contests this last point.[67] Marshall thinks the function of water baptism in Acts is specifically to relate the experience of the individual to that of the church. In any case, Giles and Marshall agree that baptism in Acts is a public confession of Jesus as Lord, an outward indication of the existence of faith. So also Schweizer: "For Luke baptism is simply a natural episode in what he regards as much more important, namely conversion."[68]

G. Beasley-Murray indicates that, compared to other New Testament writings, Luke holds a "primitive" concept of baptism.[69] There is no idea, for instance, of the participation of the believer in the death and resurrection of Christ (cf. Rom 6). Baptism in Acts is performed in the name of Jesus, not in the name of the Father, Son, and Holy Spirit (Matt 28:19).

The connection of baptism to the reception of the Holy Spirit is undeveloped, as noted above (pp. 54–56). Luke seems to think that baptism and the Spirit go together (Acts 2:38; 9:17–18; 10:47–48; 19:2–6) but there are too many anomalies for this to appear as the means by which the Spirit is bestowed. Sometimes, baptism and the gift of the Spirit are intentionally separated (8:16).

If Luke's doctrine of baptism is ambiguous (or at least elusive to modern scholars), this does not mean he thinks baptism unimportant. The frequency with which he reports the event indicates he regards it as normative Christian experience.

2. *Breaking of bread.* Luke describes the Jerusalem community as gathering regularly "to break bread" (2:42, 46) and later mentions the church founded by Paul in Troas doing the same (20:7, 11).

Kevin Giles does not think this refers to the eucharist, especially since Luke uses the same expression elsewhere for a meal Paul eats with pagan sailors (27:35).[70] Likewise, James Dunn takes the references to the breaking of bread as indicative of ordinary meals, continuing Jesus' practice of table-fellowship described in Luke's gospel (e.g., 5:29; 15:2).[71]

Most scholars, however, think the references are eucharistic.[72] Jesus is described as breaking bread at the last supper in Luke's gospel (22:17), the only gospel in which Jesus is also depicted as telling his disciples to "do this in remembrance of me" (22:19). Marshall, however, notes that the brief descriptions of the breaking of bread in Acts offer a potentially different picture than we usually have of a Christian eucharist.[73] There is no mention of wine. No words of institution are spoken. And no reference is made either backward to the death of Jesus or forward to the heavenly banquet. The context for the "breaking of bread" in Acts is neither memorial nor eschatological, but existential: the meal is a joyful celebration of fellowship expressed in praise of God (2:46–47).

These distinctions led Hans Lietzmann to propose that Luke preserves an alternative tradition regarding the eucharist to that which we find in Paul—one which offered a joyful celebration of the Lord's presence rather than a solemn memorial of his death.[74] Lietzmann's thesis has been challenged.[75] The dichotomy seems unnecessary, since realizations of presence and remembrance are not mutually exclusive. In any case, Marshall notes that Luke's reader is expected to interpret the breaking of bread in Acts in light of the last supper account in the gospel (Luke 22:14–20). Here, the wine is present, the words of institution are given, and both eschatological (22:18) and memorial (22:19) aspects of the meal are stressed. The references in Acts are not intended as descriptions of the meal, but only as reports that the church is continuing to practice that which is described in the gospel.

Still, Marshall admits, the focus in the Acts accounts is on the "glad and sincere hearts" of those who partake (2:42). This may be because the eucharist is regarded as a time when the risen Lord is especially present. In Luke's gospel the risen Jesus is said to be made known to his disciples in the breaking of bread (24:35). In this regard, Joachim Wanke emphasizes the connection of the meals in chapter 2 and chapter 20 with the saving power of God.[76] In the first instance this is noted by the reference to the Lord adding to the communing party daily those who were being saved (2:47), and in the latter instance it is dramatically demonstrated in the resurrection of Eutychus (20:9–10). Even the breaking of bread among the pagan sailors in 27:35 is linked with the thought of God's saving presence (27:34).

Two further details regarding the breaking of bread in Acts are often noted: the eucharistic celebration appears to take place within the context of a full meal (cf. 1 Cor 11:17–34) and it appears to be celebrated frequently—daily in 2:46 and on the first day of each week in 20:7.

3. *Sharing possessions*. Two passages in the first portion of Acts describe the early church as practicing what some have called a form of "Christian communism." Acts 2:44–45 says, "All who believed were together and had all things in common; they would sell their possessions and goods and distribute the proceeds as any had need." Acts 4:32–37 describes the practice in more detail: the group was of one heart and soul; no one claimed private ownership of any possessions; everything they owned was held in common; there was not a needy person among them; lands and houses were sold and the proceeds laid at the apostle's feet for distribution to those in need.

Luke Johnson indicates that Luke is here reflecting a Hellenistic ideal of friendship.[77] By saying the believers were of "one heart and soul" he recalled a popular Hellenistic proverb, "Friends are one soul," and by saying that they "held all things in common" he echoed another traditional saying, "For friends, all things are common." Thus, Luke presents the Jerusalem Christians as fulfilling the Greek ideal of true friendship. At the same time, he presents them as fulfilling another ideal—that of the Old Testament, where Moses announces to the people that "if only you obey the voice of the Lord your God . . . there will not be a needy one among you" (Deut 15:4–5).

Johnson also notes that the sharing of possessions presented here in Acts does not continue to be practiced in other communities described later in the narrative. There is, accordingly, no reason to think Luke expected subsequent Christian communities to practice a strict community of goods. Rather, he offers an idealized portrait of how things were in the primordial beginning, at the founding of the community. The sketching of such an idealized paradigm is typical in Hellenistic literature. The description is not offered to teach Christians of every time and place how they ought to dispose of their possessions, but rather to say something about the church as a people whose unity is given by the Spirit.

Walter Pilgrim treats the texts a little less symbolically, though he too admits the specifics are not intended as a mandate for all time.[78] The real emphasis in these passages is on the ongoing charity that is expected to remain a part of Christian community always and everywhere. The texts are misread if it is assumed that all of the Jerusalem Christians were required to sell all of their goods and pool their resources. For one thing, the selling of goods is done voluntarily—otherwise the generous gift of Barnabas (4:36–37) would not be worthy of note. In addition, Luke depicts the selling of possessions to meet community needs as an ongoing process rather than as a one-time total divestment. He envisions a community where everyone is concerned about everyone else and willing to part with their possessions on behalf of others when the need requires. This ideal *is* repeated in Acts, on an even grander scale. When a famine spreads throughout the world and Palestine is hit especially hard, the church in Antioch of Syria makes provisions to help its suffering neighbors in Jerusalem (11:27–30).

Observations and Conclusions

The matters discussed in this chapter are closely related to those discussed in the last one. Luke's understanding of God, Jesus, and the Holy Spirit definitely affect his vision of the church and its ministry. The reverse may also be true: Luke is a pastoral theologian who has worked out his ideas concerning subjects discussed in the last chapter within the context of concerns we have just examined.

Such a connection can also be seen with regard to eschatology and ecclesiology. Although scholars disagree on their assessments of both subjects in the Lukan writings, they agree that the two topics are related. For example, scholars who think Luke views the parousia as both future and delayed are likely to ascribe to him a more schematized system of church leadership, a more defined program of evangelism, a more intentional effort at achieving rapport with the state, and a more institutional pattern of congregational life. It makes sense for a church that believes it is in the world "for the long haul" to settle down and attend to such matters.

By contrast, scholars who believe Luke either expects an imminent end or thinks the salvation associated with the end has already come are more likely to read his conception of the church as charismatic, undefined, and even haphazard at times. The urgency of the mission or the certainty of divine aid relativizes concerns for precision in ecclesiastical matters.

We have observed in previous chapters that Luke-Acts is often read either in terms of salvation history or in terms of promise and fulfillment. At the risk of over-simplifying, we can now remark that the salvation history model tends to approach the issue of eschatology as a question of whether the parousia will be delayed or imminent (will the Age of the Church be long or short?). The promise and fulfillment model tends to approach the issue of eschatology as a question of whether God's promises are to be fulfilled in the present or in the future.

Thus, once a Lukan scholar adopts either the salvation history or the promise and fulfillment model for understanding these books, he or she is committed to answering an essential question regarding eschatology. The answer to that question will, in turn, significantly influence the understanding of Luke's concept of the church and related matters.

In practice, however, many scholars are eclectic or even inconsistent in their approach to Luke-Acts. Scholars, like most people, do not like to be categorized.

5
Reading Acts as History

Unless instructed otherwise, the average person who picks up the book of Acts probably reads it as the history book of the early church.[1] Most scholars, however, do not read Acts in this way. As our last two chapters have demonstrated, the main interest of recent scholarship has been in the theological teaching of Acts rather than in its historical information.

Still, Acts remains the only record for much of what happened during this formative period and a number of Lukan scholars maintain that Acts should be given more credit for its historical contributions. The title of I. H. Marshall's book, *Luke: Historian and Theologian*, indicates his opinion that Luke deserves to be taken seriously in both of the capacities named.[2]

Two questions are of significance in reading Acts as history: 1) How does Luke compare with other historians of his own day? 2) How can the book of Acts be used as a source for writing church history today? We will first examine answers that have been given to both of these questions and will then survey the results of scholarship that has attempted to read the book of Acts as history.

Luke Among the Ancients

Some scholars do not believe Luke ever intended to write history. Richard Pervo regards Acts as a historical novel, that is, as a work that may contain some historical information but is intended primarily to entertain and to edify (see above, pp. 11-13).[3] Many scholars, however, believe that Luke at least wants to be taken seriously as a historian. Attention is drawn to features of his writings that give them the appearance of historical accounts: the stereotypical prefaces in Luke 1:1–4 and Acts 1:1–5; the claim to rely on eyewitness testimony (Luke 1:2; Acts 1:3; and the "we sections" of Acts); the numerous speeches presented in Acts. All these give the book "the stamp of a historical writing."[4]

Of course, Acts is not a work of history in the modern sense. Luke does not identify his sources and he fails to maintain a critical distance from his subject matter. Still, it would be unfair to decide whether Luke deserves to be respected as a historian on the basis of modern expectations. The question is, what were the expectations of historians in antiquity? Bertil Gärtner answers this in part by comparing Acts to other Hellenistic Jewish writings, especially the books of 1 and 2 Maccabees.[5] These works show that it was acceptable for a historian of this age to interpret all events, as Luke does, from a religious standpoint. Victories and defeats are ultimately traced back to the intervention of God. Eckhardt Plümacher takes a different approach in his monograph, *Lukas als hellenistischer Schriftsteller.* He compares Acts to Greek authors, especially Livy.[6] He notices many similar tendencies, including the use of an archaizing style for speeches and of a dramatic episode style for narrative. Plümacher concludes that, in many ways, Luke's work may be regarded as typical of ancient Hellenistic historiography.

W. C. van Unnik explores this theme from another angle in his article, "Luke's Second Book and the Rules of Hellenistic Historiography."[7] He draws up a list of rules historians in Luke's day were expected to follow, according to two ancient writings: the Roman Antiquities of Dionysius of Halicarnassus, written between 30–37 B.C., and an essay by Lucian of Samosate, written between A.D. 166–168. Dionysius evaluates a number of historians according to certain standards that he thinks they should meet; Lucian gives outright instruction on "How To Write History." Since the book of Acts was written between the times when these two works were composed, it can be evaluated according to their criteria to determine what Luke's contemporaries would have thought of his work.

Dionysius thinks the first task of any historian should be to choose a "good subject of a lofty character" that will be truly profitable to its reader. He criticizes one ancient writer, Thucydides, for writing of a single war, which "should not have happened or (failing that) should have been ignored by posterity and consigned to silence and oblivion." Likewise, Lucian says that the subject should be "important, essential, close to home, or of practical utility." In short, history should be useful. Van Unnik thinks Acts fulfills this criterion, for Luke makes it clear that what he reports has lasting significance for all the earth (1:8; 10:36–42; 13:46–48; 26:26). Furthermore, his writings are intended to fulfill the practical need of offering their reader certainty concerning what has been heard (Luke 1:4).

Both Dionysius and Lucian are concerned with how a work of history should be structured. Lucian emphasizes that there should be a clear sequence to the order of presentation. Dionysius stresses that the work should begin and end appropriately. Van Unnik thinks Luke passes this point with honors. The book begins with a commission to the apostles to be witnesses to the ends of the earth (1:8) and then proceeds, sequentially, to trace the progress of the gospel to new areas: Jerusalem, Samaria, Caesarea, Antioch, Asia Minor, Greece, Rome. In this light, the ending, too, is appropriate. We may want to know more about what happened to Paul after he reached Rome, but Luke's simple report of his preaching there indicates that the goals of mission as set forth within this work (19:21) have been fulfilled.

In other matters, Dionysius and Lucian offer advice that might be rejected by historians today. Both advise historians to write with rapidity, omitting information that is not central to the significant points. In addition, the historian should write with a vividness that arouses the reader's emotions to compassion or anger. Luke does all this in Acts, sometimes to the chagrin of modern critics. Today's scholars consider his lack of detail concerning the organization of the early church and his omission of information concerning other apostles to be major gaffes. Likewise, the lively appearance of his stories and the skillful variety with which they are told lead some to believe he is more interested in achieving dramatic effects and pathos than in presenting an account of history. Yet van Unnik argues that in these matters Luke is doing precisely what would be expected of him, as a historian in his own day.

Other items noted by van Unnik include Luke's paucity of topographical details and his introduction of speeches designed to fit both the speaker and the occasion. These considerations convince van Unnik that Luke must be regarded as a competent historian within the framework of his own age. Luke "knew the rules of the game and was capable of applying them with propriety."

To say that Luke was a competent historian for his own day does not necessarily imply that his work holds any merit by today's standards. Some scholars would say that, granted Luke's integrity as an ancient historian, the lack of concern for truth that characterized modern historiography still disqualifies Acts from being taken seriously as history today.[8] Van Unnik, however, contests this point as well. Another feature that both Dionysius and Lucian emphasize in their "rules for Hellenistic historiography" is a commitment to telling the truth. Historians who are easily swayed by flattery or bribery, for instance, are to be rejected. Historians, even in ancient times, were expected to be honest.[9]

Acts as a Resource for Church History

In his work *Luke the Historian*, C. K. Barrett describes the dilemma faced by modern interpreters who wish to use Acts as a resource for church history.[10] For Luke, history could not be divorced from preaching. Luke relates the history that he believes contains the gospel, and in doing so he offers us two pictures of the church. He sets out to depict the church of the first decades, but unconsciously depicts also the church of his own time. He does this by selecting and arranging materials that he believes will proclaim the message he wants his church to hear. He does so also by reading back into the past the assumptions and presuppositions of his own time. Thus, his work gives us the "impression of a screen upon which two pictures are being projected at the same time—a picture of the church of the first period, and, superimposed upon it, a picture of Luke's own times."

Barrett emphasizes that it is not to Luke's discredit that he has done this. Nevertheless, historians who are interested in the picture of the earliest church must work to distinguish what Luke offers concerning that period, from what actually reflects his own period. Gerd Lüdemann has produced a commentary on the entire book of Acts that attempts to do this.[11] He calls his book *Early Christianity according to the Traditions in Acts*. Lüdemann's method, widely accepted among scholars,[12] is to begin by separating what he calls "tradition" from what he calls "redaction." Tradition here refers to that which derives ultimately from Luke's sources, oral or written. Redaction refers to that which derives from Luke's own editorial activity. Since Lüdemann does not believe Luke himself was a witness to any of these events (including those reported in the so-called "we passages"), the question of the historical value of Acts is in reality a question of the historical value of the traditions incorporated into Acts. That which can be identified as redaction can be dismissed for historical purposes—it reflects Luke's own perspective.

The task of separating tradition and redaction is difficult. Lüdemann admits that Luke has integrated his sources so carefully into his work that linguistic and stylistic peculiarities are only rarely fruitful in identifying source material. Most of the time, Lüdemann identifies as redaction that material which seems to serve Luke's own particular purposes. For example, in Acts 18:12–17, the mention of Paul's preaching every sabbath in the synagogue probably derives from Luke's interest in presenting Paul as an exemplary Jew. The positive portrait of Gallio reflects Luke's interest in demonstrating how Romans ought to behave toward Christians. These concerns are recurring themes in Luke's gospel and in Acts—the sort of themes that Luke might have introduced for the benefit of the church in his own day.

Even traditional material might be historically worthless. After separating tradition from redaction, Lüdemann evaluates the tradition according to certain historical criteria. He rejects as historical all reports of the miraculous or supernatural. The healing of the lame man in 3:1–10 is no doubt traditional, but "those who are lame from their childhood are (unfortunately) not made whole again."

The principal means for seeking confirmation of traditional material, however, is comparison with other sources. Sometimes, of course, the information is unique and then a final judgment of its veracity might have to be suspended. Much of the time, however, we are able to ask whether the tradition Luke preserves "fits" with what we know about the Roman world from other writings or with what we know about Paul from his own letters. Lüdemann does not expect exact correspondences—if that were the case, Acts would, by definition, tell us nothing we don't already know. Rather, he asks whether this information is compatible with the general picture gained elsewhere. For example, Acts 21:21 mentions a hostile rumor to the effect that Paul taught Jews to forsake Moses. This is certainly to be classed as tradition, since Luke's own concern is to present Paul as a law-abiding Jew who gets along well with other Christians. The tradition, furthermore, is probably historical because some statements in Paul's letters (Gal 2:11–19; 5:6; 6:15; 1 Cor 7:19) make it easy to see how such a rumor could have started.

It has become axiomatic in Pauline studies to treat Acts as subservient to the letters. As Richard Jeske puts it, "The proper procedure is to begin with the data from Paul and to utilize the data from Acts, after critical assessment, alongside the Pauline scheme."[13] Günther Bornkamm notes in the introduction to his highly-respected biography of Paul that he draws on Acts only with "great restraint."[14]

Lüdemann's similarly restrained approach discovers much in Acts that *is* historical. In general, though, he finds Luke is better at preserving individual facts than at chronology or synthesis. Luke often brings various stories about one geographical place together in the narrative without regard for their historical sequence. Still, once a chronological framework has been devised through analysis of Paul's letters, information derived from the traditions incorporated into Acts can be used to augment our understanding of early Christianity.

Colin Hemer, in his study, *The Book of Acts in the Setting of Hellenistic History*, follows a methodology different from that of Lüdemann.[15] Because Hemer regards the author of Acts as a companion of Paul and, therefore, an eyewitness of much that he reports, there is little need to distinguish "tradition" from "redaction." The bigger question is whether Luke is telling the truth. We should check his accuracy on those matters where it can be checked and thus gain a perspective for evaluating claims that cannot be verified. Following this approach, Hemer finds himself able to affirm the historicity of Acts to a much greater extent than Lüdemann.

The Historical Value of Material in *Acts*

Whichever methodology is used to gain a historical reading of Acts, scholars end up comparing the material in Acts to evidence drawn from other sources. In general, three different types of material are discerned: that which is confirmed historically by other sources; that which is unparalleled by other sources; and that which contradicts or is in tension with other sources.

1. *Material confirmed by other sources.* Adrian N. Sherwin-White, a historian of the Roman Empire and a specialist in matters of Roman law and administration, recognizes that the book of Acts is a "propaganda narrative," liable to distortion.[16] Nevertheless, he finds that in matters related to geography, politics, law, and administration, "the confirmation of historicity is overwhelming." For example, Acts correctly identifies the chief magistrates of Philippi as "praetors" who are attended by "lictors" (16:35), while at Thessalonica, the city authorities are identified as "politarchs" (17:6). Sherwin-White thinks it absurd for biblical scholars to question the historicity of Acts with regard to such details. Roman historians, he avers, have long taken the book's accuracy on these matters for granted. Similarly, Gordon Hewart regards the book of Acts as offering the best available "picture of the *Pax Romana* and all that it meant—good roads and posting, good police, freedom from brigandage and piracy, freedom of movement, toleration, and justice."[17] A recent study by Harry Tajra focuses specifically on the details of Paul's trials before Roman officials in the second half of Acts and confirms the essential accuracy in the treatment of such matters as legal terminology, penal procedure, and state institutions.[18] Martin Hengel notes further that many obscure details about the Roman world as described in Acts are confirmed in the writings of the Jewish-Roman historian, Josephus.[19] An example would be the references in Acts to certain obscure rebels (5:36–37; 21:38), whose deeds are also mentioned by Josephus.

In matters of background, then, Acts is deemed remarkably

accurate.[20] This, as W. Ward Gasque notes, is even more notewor-
thy when it is remembered that Luke did not have access to all of
the research tools available in libraries today.[21] He manages to give
correct information regarding the historical details of an age before
his time and of geographical regions not his own. How? He must
have had access to reliable information (either through written
sources or through personal experience) and the inclination to
convey this information faithfully.

Acts also offers a number of details about the life of Paul that
agree with information provided by Paul's own letters. Gerhard
Krodel gives the following list:[22] a) Paul persecuted Christians prior
to becoming a Christian himself (9:1–2; Gal 1:13; 1 Cor 15:9); b)
Paul had been a Pharisee "zealous for the traditions" of his Jewish
ancestors (22:3; 23:6; Phil 3:4–8; Gal 1:14); c) Paul was once smug-
gled out of Damascus by being lowered over the wall of the city in
a basket (9:23–25; 2 Cor 11:32–33); d) Paul went to Syria and
Cilicia after his first visit to Jerusalem (9:30; Gal 1:21); e) Paul
worked with Barnabas in Antioch (11:25; Gal 1:21, 2:1); f) Paul
met with persecution in Antioch, Iconium, and Lystra (13—14; 2
Tim 3:11; cf. 2 Cor 11:25); g) Paul did not require Gentile Christians to be circumcised (15; Gal 1—2); h) Paul took Silas and
Timothy with him on a missionary journey after quarreling with
Barnabas in Antioch (15:39–40; 16:3; Gal 2:13; 1 Thess 1:1); i)
Paul established churches in Philippi, Thessalonica, Athens, Corinth, and Ephesus (16—19; 1 Thess 1:1; 2:2; 3:1 and the other
Pauline letters). He was treated shamefully in Philippi and met
with opposition in Thessalonica (16:22; 17:5; 1 Thess 2:2); j) Paul
supported himself financially by working with his own hands (18:3;
20:33–35; 1 Thess 2:9; 1 Cor 4:12; 9:18); k) Paul met Priscilla and
Aquila in Corinth and Ephesus (18:1–3, 18; 1 Cor 16:19; 2 Tim
4:19; Rom 16:3). In addition to these aspects of Paul's own biography, details about other persons in Acts are sometimes confirmed
by information in Paul's letters: e.g., the ministry of Apollos in
Ephesus and Corinth (18:24–28; 1 Cor 16:12) and the role of James
in leading the Jerusalem church (15; 20; 21:17–26; Gal 2:9).

Though this list is impressive, some scholars note minor discrepancies with regard to these matters. In his letters, Paul speaks
of his life as a Pharisee in the past tense (Gal 1:13–14; Phil 3:4–8),

but in Acts Paul claims he still is a Pharisee (22:3; 23:6). In 2 Corinthians 11:32–33, Paul describes the basket episode in Damascus as an escape from "the governor under King Aretas," whereas Acts 9:23–25 describes it as an escape from "the Jews." The reason for the quarrel between Paul and Barnabas given in Acts 15:36–40 is quite different from that offered by Paul in Galatians 2:11–13. Still, it can be said that, in many ways, Luke's account of Paul's life can be confirmed by information provided by Paul's own epistles.

2. *Material that is unparalleled*. The vast majority of information offered in the book of Acts is neither confirmed nor contested by other sources. Scholars disagree widely as to how to regard this material with respect to historicity. F. F. Bruce says that since Luke usually gets the facts straight in those instances where he can be checked, he has earned "the right to be treated as a reliable informant on matters . . . not corroborated elsewhere."[23] Likewise, I. H. Marshall thinks that "a writer who is careful to get the background right may be expected to tell a reliable story as well."[24] Hans Conzelmann, however, objects to this reasoning, according to what he calls his "Karl May rule." An accurate description of milieu, Conzelmann says, "proves nothing at all relative to the historicity or 'exactness' of the events told."[25] For on that basis, "one can prove even the historicity of the stories of Karl May" (a German novelist who wrote about American Indian culture).[26] Similarly, Henry Cadbury admits that what we read in Acts generally conforms to what we know of the history and culture of the first-century world, but he also notes that Greek and Latin novels are often as full of accurate and local contemporary color as are historical writings.[27]

The unparalleled material in Acts is of different types. First, as Gerhard Krodel points out, Luke offers a great deal of incidental information that is otherwise unknown to us.[28] Outside of Acts, we would never have heard of Matthias (1:23–26), Aeneas (9:33), Tabitha (9:36), Agabus (11:28; 21:10), Rhoda (12:13), Lydia (16:4), Jason (17:7), Damaris (17:34), or of the three different persons named Ananias (5:1; 9:10; 23:2). Acts also offers detailed information regarding the times and places for Paul's visits to various locations. Although it is impossible to verify such details, many scholars find the concrete nature of the information convincing in itself. It is not the sort of material a writer would invent. In addition, Krodel notes that such details are not found everywhere. The account of Paul's first missionary journey (13—14) lacks the precise references that are found later in the "we sections." This indicates that Luke only cited names and places "when he knew them."

Another type of unparalleled material in Acts involves information that is similar to but more specific than information found elsewhere. Paul claims to belong to the tribe of Benjamin (Rom 11:1; Phil 3:5); Acts says his given name was "Saul" (7:58), the name of the most illustrious member of that tribe. Paul says he was trained as a Pharisee (Phil 3:5; Gal 1:14); Acts says his teacher was Gamaliel, one of the greatest Pharisees of the day (22:3). Paul says he persecuted the church violently (Gal 1:13); Acts says he had Christians put to death (22:4; 26:10). Paul speaks of the gospel as the power of God for salvation "to the Jew first and also to the Greek" (Rom 1:16); Acts depicts Paul as always preaching first to Jews in synagogues and only subsequently turning to Gentiles (13:44–46; 28:23–28). Some scholars regard these statements in Acts as partially verified by the information in Paul's letters and, therefore, as likely to be accurate.[29] Others, however, suspect that Luke is developing traditions that he knew only in vague or fragmentary form: he "spins off" new details and even entire stories from bits and pieces of data available to him.[30]

A third type of unparalleled material in Acts includes accounts that strike many scholars as inherently nonhistorical, such as tales that are overly literary, adventurous, or miraculous. Ernst Haenchen notes Luke's dramatic technique of "scene writing": when he is "untrammelled by tradition," he enjoys a freedom that we would grant only to the historical novel.[31] A good example is the extended account of Paul's sea voyage and shipwreck in Acts 27—28. Although the details of the route may be historical and although Paul himself says in 2 Corintians 11:25 that he was shipwrecked (three times!), the story told here may be a literary construction. Even F. F. Bruce, who thinks it is based on the author's personal recollection, admits that the form of the story goes back to Homer's *Odyssey* with some dependence on the Old Testament voyage of Jonah.[32] As for stories involving the miraculous, judgments regarding historicity usually depend on the predispositions of the interpreter.[33] Lüdemann, we have seen, excludes the supernatural from historical consideration outright.[34] Many scholars regard the miracle stories in Acts as a crude attempt to represent the power of the Spirit as operative in the apostles. Others see the miracle tales as Lukan spin-offs of statements like that of Paul in 2 Corinthians 12:12. Some, of course, have no *a priori* reason to doubt that such events happened just as Luke describes them.

In conclusion, material that is unparalleled in Acts is generally tested by scholars to determine its probable historicity. Concrete detail is usually rated high while especially literary accounts tend to be rated low. Partial correspondence with other traditions is interpreted positively by some scholars but negatively by others. The overriding consideration for evaluating the historicity of unparalleled material, however, is the question of whether the material appears to serve Luke's own agenda: if it does, its historicity is immediately suspect. On this basis, the identification of Paul as being from Tarsus (21:39; 22:3) is usually accepted as historical, for it serves no redactional purpose. The identification of Paul as a Roman citizen (16:37–39; 22:25–29) is more likely to be questioned, since this serves Luke's purpose of furthering peaceful relations between Christians and Rome.[35]

3. *Material in tension with other sources.* Some material in Acts appears to contradict what is expressed elsewhere, such as in Paul's letters. An obvious example of such a contradiction can be seen by comparing Paul's own account of his visits to Jerusalem in Galatians 1—2 with that offered by Luke in Acts 9, 11, and 15.[36] Paul insists in Galatians 1:15–24 that he did not visit Jerusalem until three years after his "call" (conversion) and that he saw no apostles except Peter and James at that time. He was not "known by sight to the churches in Judea" and he did not return to Jerusalem for fourteen years (2:1). This is a matter of great importance for Paul, probably because he wants to make it clear that his ministry was not in any way authorized by or under the authority of the apostles in Jerusalem. He swears, "in what I am writing to you, before God, I do not lie!" In Acts, however, Paul is presented to the apostles by Barnabas (9:27). He goes "in and out among them at Jerusalem, preaching boldly" (9:28–29). He appears to have a

close relationship with the Christians there, and they appear to play some role in determining his movements. They "bring" him to Caesarea and "send" him to Tarsus (9:30).

Even greater discrepancies become apparent when Paul's account of a later meeting with the apostles in Jerusalem (Gal 2:1–10) is compared with Luke's account in Acts 15:1–35. To begin with, Paul insists that this is only his second visit to the city, but according to Acts it would be his third (11:30; 12:25). In any case, both Galatians and Acts describe the purpose of the meeting as being to settle the question of whether Gentile converts must be expected to obey the law of Moses. In Galatians, Paul reports that "nothing was added" and that he was encouraged to continue his law-free mission to Gentiles. In Acts, however, the council decrees that Gentiles must keep certain requirements and Paul is given the task of promulgating these restrictions.

Numerous theories have been proposed to resolve these tensions.[37] Colin Hemer favors a popular view suggesting that Galatians 2 and Acts 15 do not refer to the same event: the council described in Acts 15 took place at a later period, after the letter to the Galatians had been written.[38] Martin Hengel points to evidence for such dating in what appears to be a variant tradition incorporated into the book of Acts itself: in Acts 21:25 Luke portrays Paul being told about the decree in a way that implies he has not heard of it before.[39] Whatever reconstruction is given, however, historical problems remain. F. F. Bruce, who has a very high regard for the historical accuracy of Acts, decides that the accounts in Galatians and those in Acts are "impossible to harmonize."[40] Paul Achtemeier regards these discrepancies as evidence that the purpose of Acts and its value for us today does not lie in its detailed historical accuracy but in its theological points (see above, pp. 13–14).[41]

Philipp Vielhauer alleges that Luke misrepresents Paul not only biographically but also theologically (see above, pp. 35–36).[42] For example, in the Areopagus speech of Acts 17:22–31, Paul is represented as espousing a friendly attitude toward pagan religion and as proclaiming the gospel in terms derived from Stoic philosophy. He does not mention the cross but appeals to his Greek audience with words of human wisdom. The real Paul, Vielhauer

insists, would have preached Christ crucified (1 Cor 1:22–24).
Here the gospel is forsaken for "natural theology." As Albert
Schweitzer puts it, the Pauline emphasis on being in Christ by
grace is replaced by a pagan emphasis on being in God by nature.[43]

Bertil Gärtner, however, argues that the Areopagus speech is
not incompatible with Pauline theology.[44] Paul is merely represented as seeking points of contact in order to gain a hearing. The
basic ideas of this speech are the same as those presented in Romans 1—3, the essential difference being that in Romans Paul is
writing to Christians and in Acts he is addressing pagans.

Vielhauer also objects to Luke's representation of Paul's attitude toward the law. The historical Paul, Vielhauer says, leveled a
polemic against the law, declaring that Christ was the "end of the
law" (Rom 10:4). But in Acts, Luke portrays Paul as utterly loyal
to the law. The Paul who wrote in Galatians, "If you receive circumcision, Christ will be of no advantage to you" (5:2) is actually
described in Acts as circumcising Timothy (16:3). Gasque, however, defends the Lukan portrait.[45] Paul was not anti-law, but anti-
legalism. The argument in Galatians is directed toward persons
who teach circumcision as necessary for salvation.

Vielhauer makes two further objections to the Lukan portrait
of Paul's theology. With regard to christology, Paul in Acts does
not make reference to either the preexistence of Christ or to the
saving effect of Jesus' death on the cross (except for 20:28). And,
finally, with regard to eschatology, Paul is not presented in Acts as
one who lives in the imminent expectation of the end. Gasque
accepts these points as essentially valid, but thinks them less devas-
tating to the historical veracity of Luke's narrative than Vielhauer
imagines. Acts presents only a few representative sermons of Paul,
not an exhaustive account of his theology. The fact that he omits
certain major motifs should not call into question the accuracy of
what he does present.

F. F. Bruce approaches the differences between Paul in his
own letters and Paul in Acts from another perspective.[46] In Acts,
Bruce says, Paul is consistently depicted as more adaptable than he
appears to be in his letters. In the Areopagus speech he strives to
be accommodating to Greeks, and in circumcising Timothy he
strives to be accommodating to Jews. This tendency appears some-

what exaggerated in Acts, but Paul himself does say in 1 Corinthians that he has become all things to all people: "To those under the law, I became as one under the law . . . that I might win those under the law. To those outside the law, I became as one outside the law . . . that I might win those outside the law" (9:19–22). So the Lukan concept of an adaptable Paul is not entirely without warrant.

Like Gasque, Bruce also stresses that the Lukan Paul is distinctive mainly due to omissions. The quarrel with Peter in Antioch (Gal 2:11–14) is absent here, as is any reference to the painful relations Paul had with the church in Corinth. Acts "tends to pass over fundamental controversies in silence and to emphasize the things that make for peace."

Bruce also explains the distinctive portrait of Paul in Acts with reference to two other points. First, echoing Gärtner, Bruce stresses that letters addressed to Christians should not be expected to represent Paul in the same way as speeches addressed to unbelievers. The differences in genre and audience are significant. Only once in Acts is Paul described as speaking to Christians (20:18–35) and, notably, it is in this address that his words come closest to what we expect of him in the letters. He speaks of faith and grace (20:21, 24, 32) and he refers (only here) to the saving efficacy of Christ's death (20:28).

A second point Bruce makes is that allowance should be made for the differences between first-party and third-party perspectives when comparing the Paul of the letters and the Paul of Acts. Likewise, I. H. Marshall notes, "a man's self-portrait will not necessarily agree with the impression of him received by other people."[47]

In consideration of points like these, Jacob Jervell has challenged the basic tendency in New Testament studies to evaluate Acts from the perspective of Paul's letters but not to make judgments the other way around.[48] Acts offers us a glimpse of an otherwise "unknown Paul." In the letters, Paul is always arguing or dealing with the particular questions or problems of a specific church. "What about the unpolemical Paul?" Jervell asks. "What about all those aspects of his preaching that nobody objected to?" If there is one thing Paul's letters make clear, it is that Paul was a complex personality. Luke's view of Paul is admittedly one-sided, but that does not mean it is incorrect. Luke records a side of Paul that Paul himself sometimes displayed: a Jewish, law-observant Paul who is also a visionary, charismatic preacher, healer and miracle worker. In short, "that which lies in the shadow in Paul's letters Luke has placed in the sun." The picture of Paul in Acts is a completion, a filling-up of what we have in the letters. In order to get at the historical Paul, we cannot do without Acts.

Observations and Conclusions

We have observed that, although today the book of Acts is studied primarily for its theology, interest in reading it as history is still alive and well. Even scholars who view Acts as a history book, however, differ in their methodological approaches to evaluating the history it contains. These differences are often a product of varying views concerning such matters as authorship and sources. A scholar who believes the author of Acts was a companion of Paul and, so, an eyewitness to some of the events will naturally treat the book differently than scholars who cannot accept this.

Scholars also reach different conclusions regarding the reliability of what is reported in Acts. Lüdemann believes the book contains numerous facts, but is frequently mistaken in its chronology. Krodel thinks Luke is good on detail but sometimes misses the big picture. Bruce and Gasque admit that Luke leaves out much that is significant, but stress the accuracy of what is reported.

In 1978, A. J. Mattill discerned three contemporary views among scholars as to the use of Acts as a source for the study of Paul[49]: some scholars downplay discrepancies and argue that the Paul of Acts is basically consistent with the Paul of the letters; some contend that both the letters and Acts present one-sided views of Paul and that both are therefore necessary for historical completeness; some insist that Acts is unreliable and must be constantly tested and corrected by the letters. We have seen examples of all three of these views.

Mattill also noted what he believed was a tendency for scholars who espoused the first and the third views to cautiously accept the second. In other words, he believed there was increasing acceptance of the idea that Acts offers important, though incomplete information of a historical nature. Jacob Jervell is one scholar we have noted who has made such a move.

Finally, we should note that the subject of this chapter has been finding history in Acts, not placing Acts in history.[50] Space does not permit discussion of the numerous archaeological[51] and social-historical[52] works that enhance our knowledge of the world in which Luke's story of the early church transpires.

6
Reading Acts as Literature

Luke is a masterful storyteller and the book of Acts well displays his art. Where else within so few pages, E. J. Goodspeed once observed, "will be found such a varied series of exciting events—trials, riots, persecutions, escapes, martyrdoms, voyages, shipwrecks, rescues?"[1]

A few scholars, we observed in our first chapter, take Luke's literary finesse as evidence of scant concern with history. The book is more romance than historiography and should be interpreted as belonging to the genre of the ancient novel (see above, pp. 11–13). But scholars who read Acts as a novel are not the only ones impressed by the work's literary qualities.[2] Regardless of the value ascribed to Acts' historical witness, the book has obvious literary merit.

Literary appreciation is not divorced from concern for theological interpretation. Bible scholars do not read Acts as literature just to evaluate the book aesthetically. They try to elucidate the theological message of Acts in terms of its literary signals and effects. In recent years, New Testament scholarship has seen an influx of literary critical methodologies that attempt to interpret biblical texts according to systems traditionally used for secular literature.[3] Two approaches in particular have been used for the study of Acts: rhetorical criticism and narrative criticism.[4]

Rhetorical Criticism

Rhetorical criticism attempts to discern the means by which a work of literature achieves its particular effects on its intended readers.[5] The discipline is at least as old as Aristotle, who classified different species of rhetoric and listed types of arguments and proofs that may be used in the art of persuasion. Modern literary critics have continued this interest in analyzing a work's communicative strategy and have increasingly emphasized the need to identify the situation of the audience in order to do this effectively.[6]

With regard to Acts, rhetorical criticism has been applied mainly to the speeches, in order to determine the communication strategy used by the speaker in each particular situation. George Kennedy, a classicist, relates the speeches in Acts to Aristotle's categories.[7] A pattern can be observed in many speeches that moves from what Aristotle called "judicial rhetoric" to what he called "deliberative rhetoric." Judicial rhetoric seeks to persuade the audience to make some judgment about events occurring in the past; its typical features are accusation and defense. Deliberative rhetoric seeks to persuade them to take some action in the future; its typical feature is advice.[8] Thus, Peter in his Pentecost sermon defends the spirit-filled Christians against the charge of drunkenness (2:14–21), indicts the Jews for killing Jesus (2:22–36) and then advises his audience to repent and be baptized (2:38–39). The same pattern occurs in the speech following the healing of the lame man in 3:12–26. After accusing the Jews of Jerusalem of killing "the Author of Life," Peter suggests that they "repent therefore and turn again."

From a literary standpoint, the most interesting feature of these speeches is the loose relationship of the rhetorical argument to the situation or exigency that calls for the speech in the first place. The exigency of the first example cited above is the bewilderment of a crowd in response to a public display of glossolalia. In the second example it is astonishment over a miraculous healing. But Peter does not dwell long on these events in either case. Rather, he moves quickly to his indictment for sin and recommendation of repentance. Kennedy believes the single most important rhetorical feature of the speeches in Acts is the way the speakers consistently utilize diverse occasions to preach the gospel. Whenever an opportunity to speak arises, they try to transform the situation into an opportunity to proclaim the message of Jesus and to convert their hearers to his cause.

Burton Mack has also analyzed Peter's Pentecost sermon from the standpoint of rhetorical criticism.[9] He finds that the speech follows forms of rhetorical persuasion but in reality is not very persuasive. Peter holds that the people speaking in tongues cannot be drunk because it is only nine o'clock in the morning. Therefore, what is happening must be the work of the Spirit, as prophesied in Joel. Peter also attempts to establish a connection between Psalm 16:8–11 and the resurrection of Jesus by pointing out that the psalm cannot refer to David. Such reliance on mainly negative arguments do not sustain logically the conclusions that Peter wishes to draw. Accordingly, Mack says, the speech would only be convincing to those who were already convinced. The reported response of the audience (2:41) verifies Peter's words for Luke's readers in a way that transcends concern for logic. In short, the Pentecost sermon, within its narrative context, may be an effective communication between Luke and his readers but, apart from that context, it would have been ineffective as a communication between Peter and the Jews of Jerusalem.

Marcel Dumais comes to quite different conclusions regarding another speech in Acts, namely that of Paul delivered to the Jews in a synagogue at Pisidian Antioch (13:16–41).[10] Here, Paul is described as first gaining the confidence of his audience before presenting them with new ideas. This approach recognizes the rhetorical principle that effective argumentation must always proceed from an established "community of minds."[11] The first part of Paul's speech is devoted to recognizing the "precomprehension" of the audience. Paul selects specific presuppositions that he shares with his audience (ignoring presuppositions that he does not share with them) and uses these as the basis for presenting his case. The new proposition that Jesus is the Messiah is thus presented as a fulfillment of the history and of the prophecies that both speaker and audience accept. Paul effects this "fusion of horizons" between the precomprehension of his listeners and the new meaning he offers by using symbolic language and polyvalent terminology. For example, he says that the God who "raised up" David (13:22) has now "raised up" Jesus (13:30), and then goes on to explain the new sense in which the term "raised up" must be understood.

Bertil Gärtner interprets Paul's Areopagus speech (17:22–31) in a similar fashion (see above, p. 92).[12] The seemingly un-Pauline concepts on which the speech is built serve a rhetorical function: Paul is trying to establish some common basis on which he can build his case. The situation here is more extreme than for the address at Pisidian Antioch, for Paul shares fewer presuppositions with these Greek pagans than he does with diaspora Jews. Still, the strategy of the speech is to establish some area of common understanding and then segue from this into the new truth of the gospel.

Finally, the defense speeches of Paul found in the latter portion of Acts (22:3–21; 23:1–6; 24:10–21; 26:2–23) have been accorded rhetorical analysis by Jerome Neyrey.[13] These speeches display many features common to forensic oratory as described in ancient rhetorical handbooks. They sometimes begin with an exordium that seeks to establish the character of the accused (22:4–5; 23:1; 26:4–5). Paul stresses his respectable social standing so that his testimony will not be dismissed as that of a common, uneducated person (cf. Acts 4:13). Paul's defense speeches also concentrate (as rhetorical handbooks recommend) on defining the main issue of the debate. Paul insists that, apart from the various charges that have been brought against him (21:38; 24:5–8), the real issue is his belief in the resurrection of Jesus (23:6; 24:21; 26:6–7). His defense consists not of challenges to the trumped-up charges, but of arguments that support the validity of his claim to be a witness to the resurrection. This last point concurs with the conclusion reached by Robert O'Toole in a redactional study of Acts 26. O'Toole determines that Luke's own interest in presenting Paul's speech before Agrippa is not so much to offer his readers a defense of Paul but, rather, to present his own defense of the Christian belief in the resurrection of the dead, realized now in Jesus.[14]

Narrative Criticism

Narrative criticism attempts to interpret stories by paying special attention to the ways in which stories are told.[15] Narrative criticism differs from rhetorical criticism (and from redaction criticism) in that the concern is not to determine the intended effect of the work on its original audience. Instead, the goal is to ascertain the effect that the work assumes it will have on a reader of any time or place—on the "implied" or "ideal" reader presupposed by the text.[16] Narrative criticism interprets literature in light of general conventions of storytelling that appear to be universal and timeless. We will note a few examples of features that seem significant.

1. *Narrator.* Two recent doctoral dissertations have attempted to describe the narrator or voice that tells the story in Acts.

Allen Walworth emphasizes that the narrator of Acts is, above all, reliable.[17] In other words, Luke does not allow the narrator to ever mislead the reader, and so the reader comes to depend upon the narrator's guidance and to trust whatever the narrator says. The fact that the narrator occasionally speaks in the first person enhances this authoritative stance by giving the reader the impression that the narrator speaks as an eyewitness.[18] Having endowed the narrator with so much authority, Luke uses his narrator to guide the reader's sympathies. Characters, for example, are described from the narrator's point of view and the distance or closeness that readers feel toward characters is a direct reflection of how the narrator regards them.

Steven Sheeley concentrates his study on the manner in which the narrator communicates with the reader.[19] The narrator provides much information that is necessary for understanding the story. For example, the narrator's comment in 23:8 about the different beliefs of Pharisees and Sadducees makes the ensuing argument between representatives of these two parties intelligible. Such information not only guides the reader's interpretation of the narrative, but also places the reader in a dependent relationship with the narrator.

2. *Point of view.* Because the narrator's voice is authoritative, it becomes the norm by which the actions and statements of characters in the narrative can be judged. Robert Tannehill stresses the importance of recognizing whether an expression represents the point of view of the narrator or that of a character.[20] The perception in 8:18 that the Holy Spirit is given through the laying on of the apostles' hands does not represent the point of view of the narrator but only that of a fallible character, Simon Magus (cf. the

discussion by Käsemann and Barrett above, pp. 55–56). At times, the reader of Acts is actually invited to compare the narrator's authoritative version of an event with another version reported from the point of view of a character. In 9:15–16, the narrator reports a commission given by the Lord to Paul through Ananias (cf. 22:14–15), but later when Paul reports receiving the commission, he describes it as received from the Lord directly (26:16–18). The reader does not suspect Paul of deceit—he has proved too trustworthy for that—but recognizes that the manner in which Paul received his commission is of little importance to him. What matters is that it came from the Lord. In other cases, comparison of the narrator's account and that of a character exposes the latter as mendacious or hypocritical. In Acts 25:14–21, the Roman ruler Festus gives King Agrippa a report of his dealings with Paul. From his account, Paul's appeal to Caesar appears to be an irrational act, but the reader knows from the narrator's report in Acts 25:1–2 that Festus intended to give Paul up to his enemies. Thanks to the authoritative guidance of the narrator, the reader is better informed than King Agrippa.

3. *Characters*. The reader of Acts learns to be attentive to the characters that are presented in the story. As Tannehill notes, persons who are going to figure significantly at some later point in the story are frequently introduced as minor characters. Thus, we initially hear of Barnabas (4:36), Steven (6:5), Philip (6:5), Saul (7:58), and James (12:17) in contexts that belie the importance they will ultimately have for the story as a whole. Acts also displays a tendency to give more personality than is customary to characters who do not figure significantly in the overall plot. This is true of Aeneas and Tabitha in 9:32–43. In the New Testament gospels recipients of healing are not usually named.

Acts also displays a penchant for what literary critics call "round characters," that is, characters whose changing or conflicting traits make them appear more real.[21] Lysias, the Roman tribune, is initially ignorant but becomes wiser as the narrative progresses (21:37–38; 22:24–28; 23:12–24); he is decisive and perceptive but is also not above shading the truth for self-protection (23:26–30). Such characters are interesting for their own sake, even apart from the "plot function" they perform in the story.

Among the most compelling characters in the book of Acts
are the disciples of Jesus, who the reader already knows from
Luke's first book. Tannehill demonstrates how the faults that these
disciples exhibited in the gospel are now overcome in the story of
Acts.[22] The improvements appear very early, as can be seen from
Peter's speech in the first chapter. Whereas before the disciples
were prone to engage in rivalry over rank (Luke 9:46; 22:24), now
they think in terms of service (Acts 1:17, 25). Previously, they were
unable to accept Jesus' death as a necessary part of God's plan
(Luke 9:45; 18:34), but now they understand that what happened
was a fulfillment of scripture (Acts 1:16). These developments are
not inexplicable, for the reader is told that Jesus spent forty days
with his disciples after the resurrection, during which time he instructed them concerning the kingdom of God (Acts 1:3) and
opened their minds to understand the scriptures (Luke 24:45).[23]

After Pentecost, these improvements become even more noticeable. The disciples' tendency to entertain premature messianic
expectations (Luke 17:22; 19:11), which did surface again briefly in
Acts 1:6, now vanishes completely. Furthermore, the disciples now
appear courageous in the face of death, as they fulfill Jesus' exhor-
tation to rejoice at persecution (Acts 5:41; cf. Luke 6:22–23).
Peter's bold confessions before the Sanhedrin (Acts 4:8–12, 19–
20; 5:29–32) contrast markedly with his denials of Jesus in the
gospel (Luke 22:54–62). Indeed, when Peter accuses the Jews of
Jerusalem of having "denied" Christ but promises them that repentance will bring forgiveness and "times of refreshing" (3:14, 19),
the reader knows he speaks from his own experience.

4. *Events.* The order in which the reader learns of events can
be significant.[24] The reader does not learn about a vision Paul had
in the temple until 22:17–21, although this event apparently occurred shortly after Paul's conversion, which is reported in chapter
9. Similarly, Paul's speech to the Ephesian elders in 20:17–38 contains a number of what Tannehill calls "reviews and previews."[25]
Paul recalls past events of his ministry, some of which we learn
about for the first time, and also refers to incidents that are still to
come in the narrative: his visit to Jerusalem and subsequent imprisonment.

Also significant in the reporting of events are instances of repetition or redundancy. Acts contains three accounts of Paul's Damascus road experience (9:1–19; 22:4–16; 26:9–18), of Peter's encounter with Cornelius (10:1–48; 11:4–17; 15:7–11), and of the apostolic decree (15:19–20, 29; 21:25). Another form of repetition involves what Tannehill calls "echoes"—the reporting of similar, parallel events. We have already noted the fairly elaborate patterns of parallelism in Acts noticed by Charles Talbert and others (see above, pp. 7–8, 26). In addition to these patterns by which entire scenes or clusters of scenes repeat patterns found elsewhere in Luke's gospel or Acts, Tannehill finds numerous instances of single verse echoes. Peter's preaching evokes exactly the same question from a crowd as did that of John the Baptist (Acts 2:37; Luke 3:10, 12, 14). The last words of Stephen in 7:59–60 reprise Jesus' prayers from the cross in Luke 23:34, 46. The leaping of the lame man in Acts 14:10 recalls that of the lame man in Acts 3:8, and both bring to mind the prophecy of Isaiah 35:6. Criticism of Peter for eating with the wrong people in Acts 11:3 recalls similar criticism levelled against Jesus in Luke 5:30; 15:2; 19:7.

Tannehill further notes that repetition in Acts can take the form of "type scenes," by which different events are reported in similar ways.[26] For example, in Acts 16—19, there are four scenes in which Christians are forcibly brought before officials or a public assembly and accused (16:19–24; 17:6–9; 18:12–16; 19:25–41). The inclusion of these four similar scenes in four consecutive chapters demonstrates a concern with the way that the outside world perceives the Christian mission and with the effects that those perceptions have on Christians.

Repetitions, Tannehill explains, serve several functions.[27] They grant emphasis to the selected material and counteract the reader's tendency to forget. They exert a persuasive effect, aid the reader in forming and revising expectations, preserve the unity of the narrative, and add a suggestive richness or "resonance" to the story.

5. *Conflict.* Tannehill regards conflict as essential to the plot of Acts.[28] The central conflict in Acts occurs within Judaism and is provoked by Jewish Christians. Near the beginning of the story, the Jewish-Christian community is viewed with favor by all people (2:47). But as the narrative continues, this favorable situation sub-

sides. First the temple authorities (4:1–2; 5:17–18), then the diaspora Jews in Jerusalem (6:9–14), and finally the Jewish people in general (6:12) are aroused to instigate a great persecution of the Christian community (8:1). The theme of partial acceptance but large-scale rejection of Christian preaching by Jewish people continues throughout the stories of Paul's missionary work.

Joseph Tyson has also studied the literary motif of conflict in his book, *The Death of Jesus in Luke-Acts*.[29] He believes there is a significant distinction between the Jewish opposition to the gospel exemplified by the chief priests and that exemplified by the Pharisees. The former are portrayed as thoroughgoing villains throughout both volumes of Luke's work. Conflict between Christians and chief priests centers on the issue of authority in the temple. In Luke's gospel, Jesus' attempt to cleanse the temple is what leads to his execution at the hands of the chief priests. In Acts, Christians seek to worship, pray, and teach in the temple, but they are consistently expelled. By contrast, Luke tries to show that there is no essential incompatibility between Christians and Pharisees. The latter are not connected with Jesus' death in the gospel and points of contrast between Pharisaic doctrine and Christian teaching are emphasized in Acts (23:6–9).

How is this conflict resolved? The concluding episode of Acts portrays Paul as preaching unfettered in Rome. He has confronted Jewish resistance there with a declaration that God's salvation has been sent to the Gentiles. Accordingly, Charles Puskas views the resolution as *triumphant*.[30] In spite of Jewish rejection, Gentiles will listen (28:28). The Jewish opposition to the gospel remains final, but this no longer matters because the Gentiles are accepting the message the Jews rejected. The final words of the narrative stress the final triumph of Christianity over religious, racial, and political obstacles. Tyson considers this resolution to be *ironic*.[31] He, too, thinks the concluding episode implies final rejection of the gospel by Jewish people, but this is ironic because the Christian message is compatible with Pharisaic belief and should have been appealing at least to the Pharisaic Jews. Tannehill thinks the plot of Acts is *tragic*.[32] From the very beginning of his two-volume work, Luke has emphasized scriptural promises of salvation for Israel (e.g., Luke 1:68–69; 2:30–32). The narrative tells the story of how

God's plan to save Israel is not fulfilled. The plot is also, therefore, open-ended. The central conflict in the narrative remains unresolved. At the end of the story, the mission to be witnesses to the ends of the earth (1:8) remains uncompleted and the promises of salvation for the Jewish people remain unfulfilled. Acts offers no solution except "the patient and persistent preaching of the gospel in hope that the situation will change."[33] (These analyses may be compared with other studies on Jews and Gentiles in Acts; see above, pp. 67–72.)

6. *Symbolism*. Literary criticism recognizes that some meanings in narrative transcend literal applications. Luke Johnson suggests that possessions function symbolically in Acts.[34] In *The Literary Function of Possessions in Luke-Acts*, he describes possessions as a metaphor for human existence or human identity: what characters do with their possessions expresses symbolically what happens to them as persons. Thus, Judas' purchase of a field (1:18) symbolizes his apostasy from the community. Other believers sell their fields in order to share possessions with all (4:34–35). The sharing of possessions is symbolic of the unity of the Holy Spirit that exists at a deeper level. Authority over possessions, furthermore, symbolizes spiritual authority. The Jerusalem Christians are described as laying their possessions at the feet of the apostles (4:35, 37) to symbolize their submission to the apostles' authority. Disposition of one's possessions is a direct symbol of the disposition of one's self. This is why the sin of Ananias and Sapphira (5:1–11) is so serious: in holding back possessions, they mock the unity of the Holy Spirit and challenge the authority of the apostles. Later, when the apostles place seven deacons over the disposition of goods (6:1–6), this symbolizes a bestowal of spiritual authority as well.

Susan Marie Praeder encourages a symbolic reading of the sea voyage narrative (Acts 27:1—28:16).[35] In this story, Paul is seen as securing the salvation of his Gentile shipmates from certain death at sea. Praeder considers this temporal salvation as symbolic of the salvation of God in Jesus Christ that Paul proclaims to Gentiles. His taking of bread and giving thanks while on board the ship (27:35) symbolizes the Christian eucharist (see above, pp. 75–77). The friendly relations with the Maltese natives and the healings

performed among them (27:1–10) represent a community experience usually associated with Christian fellowship. In short, this
account of Paul's journey to Rome, where he will be rejected by
the Jews but accepted by the Gentiles is told in a way that deliberately symbolizes the potential for the gospel to effect salvation,
faith, and fellowship in the Gentile world.

Observations and Conclusions

Literary criticism brings out nuances of meaning in texts that
traditional historical and theological studies overlook. As literary
methods are applied to Acts, scholars are able to see this work in
new light.

Both of the approaches discussed here differ from traditional
methods of biblical interpretation in that they approach the text
from the perspective of its reader rather than from the perspective
of its author. Rhetorical criticism seeks to identify the intended
effect of the text on its original readers. Narrative criticism tries to
interpret the effect of the text on implied or ideal readers of any
time and place. But neither approach is fundamentally concerned
with identifying the historical author of Acts or discerning the
sources he used in the composition of this document.

The literary approaches to Acts envision different goals than
historical interpretation. Rhetorical criticism attempts to follow
the arguments of the speeches in Acts without regard for whether
these speeches are Lukan or pre-Lukan in origin. Narrative criticism seeks to understand the flow of Luke's story without inquiring
as to whether the events of which it is comprised "really happened." Reading Acts as literature means being satisfied with the
book for its own sake, rather than treating it as a means to some
other end.

Literary critic Murray Krieger has aptly described the differences between historical and literary investigation through the
metaphors of a window and a mirror.[36] Historical studies treat texts
as windows and attempt to look through them in order to learn
something about another time and place. The text stands between
the reader and the insight that is sought and may provide the
means through which that insight is obtained. Literary criticism

regards the text as a mirror. The critic determines to look at the text, not through it, and whatever insight is gained will be found in the encounter of the reader with the text itself.

Literary criticism of the book of Acts will never replace traditional historical and theological modes of interpretation. It is unlikely that people of faith will ever be satisfied to read these stories of faith simply as stories, without wanting to inquire into the history that lies behind them. Literary criticism does not answer all the questions that people of faith ask of scripture. It does, however, answer some of those questions and, furthermore, does so in ways that other approaches cannot. For this reason, the meaning of Acts as literature will no doubt continue to be a subject for much scholarly activity.

Conclusion

Even though scholarship is divided on several basic issues regarding the interpretation of Acts, major advances have been made in understanding this book. Most of the disagreements occur within parameters that define areas of consensus.

Scholars agree that Acts can and should be read as an expression of early Christian theology, though they do not always agree in their descriptions of the theology that is expressed. For instance, scholars agree that christology is of great importance to Luke, but they disagree as to whether he represents Christ as absent or present. Likewise, scholars agree that eschatology is significant, but they disagree as to whether Luke regards the parousia as delayed or imminent or whether he thinks of eschatological salvation as present or future. Scholars agree that Luke's conception of how God is acting in history is foundational to his theology, but they disagree as to whether Luke's conception can best be described in terms of a three-stage model of salvation history or in terms of a two-stage model of promise and fulfillment. Scholars agree that Luke's ecclesiology is determined by his sense of mission, and that he thinks of this mission as both universal (inclusive of Gentiles) and Spirit-driven. They disagree, however, on the question of whether Luke believes the Spirit-led mission is still directed to Israel.

Some of these disagreements derive from fundamental questions regarding methodology. Scholars agree that it can be important to determine the theology of Acts in terms of the intentions of the book's author, but they disagree as to identification of this author—whether he was a companion of Paul and whether he was

Jewish or Gentile. Scholars agree that it is important to pay attention to the context of the world in which Acts was written, but they differ in accenting concepts from the Jewish or Hebrew environment and in emphasizing those from the Hellenistic, Greco-Roman environment. Scholars agree that Acts cannot be interpreted apart from consideration of Luke's gospel, but they differ as to the extent to which the unity of the two books should be pressed. They agree that it is important to determine the literary genre to which the book belongs, but disagree as to which genre fits best. They agree that Luke's purpose in writing Acts should be determinative for any exposition of his theology, but the variety of purposes that have been suggested lead to potentially diverse interpretations.

Scholars also agree that Acts can and should be used as a resource for reconstructing the history of early Christianity, but they disagree as to the reliability of the information it reports. Here, the disagreements often reflect differences as to the process and criteria by which the material should be evaluated. Scholars generally agree that Luke has thoroughly reshaped his sources to incorporate them into his work as a whole, but they disagree as to whether this means that tradition and redaction must be separated before historical analysis can begin. Scholars agree that there are tensions between what Luke reports and what is found, for instance, in Paul's letters, but they disagree as to the extent and significance of the discrepancies.

Finally, an increasing number of scholars agree that Acts should also be read as literature, applying the insights of modern literary method to the narrative in order to determine its intended effects on its readers. There is some disagreement, however, as to whether meaning should be sought in terms of the intended effect on the original audience or in terms of an effect on implied or ideal readers of any time or place.

Future directions for scholarship are impossible to predict, but present trends can be noted. Recent scholarship has exhibited a shift away from theological appraisal of Acts that views the book as a response to the delayed parousia, as a presentation of absentee christology, or as an attempt to establish the church as an institution grounded in world history. The newer studies have tended to emphasize Acts as a unique presentation of the gospel: by ostensibly reporting the acts of "the apostles," Luke actually proclaims the reality of *God's* saving activity in the world today. He employs categories and concepts that differ markedly from Paul or even from the other evangelists, but his intention of proclaiming what he considers to be the good news in Jesus Christ is the same. Acts, then, is to be regarded as preaching.

Recent scholarship has also exhibited a tendency to allow for more ambiguity in presentations of Luke's thought. None of the scholars discussed in this book attributes ideas to Luke that are entirely without textual support. Accordingly, there is increasing recognition that divergences of opinion concerning what Luke believes may stem from inconsistencies in the evangelist's own system. Luke is regarded more as a pastoral theologian than as a systematician.

Recent scholarship has also exhibited a tendency to become more eclectic and ecumenical. In particular, new methods of literary criticism and new insights from sociological and cultural-anthropological sciences have been brought to bear on the study of this book and of the New Testament in general. Increased contributions from women theologians and from third-world scholars continue to break new ground. Opinions on various controversial subjects are less-drawn along confessional lines than they once were.

In sum, Acts can be said to be receiving, in scholarly circles at least, the attention that it deserves. No longer regarded as a mere stepchild of the gospels, the book now attracts as much academic attention as Matthew, Mark, Luke, or John. The incorporation of readings from Acts into the three-year lectionary of the church may be a sign that Acts is gaining a better reception in the church at large also. If this is true, then church and academy may be seen as responding to the compelling attraction that this book has held for everyday Bible readers for centuries.

Notes

Introduction

    1. Ernst Haenchen, "The Book of Acts as Source Material for the History of Early Christianity," in *Studies in Luke-Acts*, ed. by L. Keck and J. Martyn, 258–78, esp. 269 (Philadelphia: Fortress Press, 1980; original, 1966).

    2. *Homilies on Acts of the Apostles*. Cited by W. Ward Gasque, *A History of the Interpretation of the Acts of the Apostles*, 2nd ed. (Peabody, MA: Hendrickson, 1989; 1st ed., 1975), 7. Gasque, however, thinks he is exaggerating.

    3. W. C. van Unnik, "Luke-Acts, a Storm Center in Contemporary Scholarship," in *Studies*, ed. by Keck and Martyn, 15–32.

    4. Mark Allan Powell, *What Are They Saying About Luke?* (New York: Paulist Press, 1989).

1. Luke's Second Volume

    1. Henry J. Cadbury, *The Making of Luke-Acts* (London: SPCK, 1958; originally published in 1927).

    2. F. F. Bruce, *The Book of the Acts*, NICNT, rev. ed. (Grand Rapids: Eerdmans, 1988), 3.

    3. Mikeal Parsons, "The Unity of Luke-Acts: Rethinking the *Opinio Communis*," in *"With Steadfast Purpose": Essays on Acts in Honor of Henry J. Flanders*, ed. by Naymond Keathley, 29–53 (Waco: Baylor University Press, 1990). Watch also for *Rethinking the Unity of Luke-Acts* by Mikeal Parsons and Richard Pervo, forthcoming from Fortress Press.

4. Robert O'Toole, *The Unity of Luke's Theology*: *An Analysis of Luke-Acts*, GNS 9 (Wilmington, DE: Michael Glazier, 1984).

5. Stephen G. Wilson, *Luke and the Law*, NTSMS 50 (Cambridge: Cambridge University Press, 1983).

6. Cadbury, *Making*, 8–9.

7. Charles H. Talbert, *Literary Patterns, Theological Themes, and the Genre of Luke-Acts*, SBLMS 20 (Missoula, MT: Scholars Press, 1974). See also Robert Morgenthaler, *Die lukanische Gesichtsschreibung als Zeugnis*: *Gestalt und Gehalt der Kunst des Lukas*, 2 vols., ATANT 14–15 (Zürich: Zwingli-Verlag, 1949); Susan Marie Praeder, "Jesus-Paul, Peter-Paul and Jesus-Peter Parallelisms in Luke-Acts: A History of Reader Response," in *SBL 1984 Seminar Papers*, ed. by K. Richards, 23–39 (Chico, CA: Scholars Press, 1984).

8. Robert C. Tannehill, *The Narrative Unity of Luke-Acts*, 2 vols. (Philadelphia and Minneapolis: Fortress Press, 1986 and 1990).

9. Stephen D. Moore, "Narrative Commentaries on the Bible: Context, Roots, and Prospects," *Forum* 3/3 (1987): 29–62. See also *Literary Criticism and the Gospels*: *The Theoretical Challenge* (New Haven: Yale University Press, 1989), 29–38.

10. James M. Dawsey, "The Literary Unity of Luke-Acts: Questions of Style—A Task for Literary Critics," *NTS* 35 (1989): 48–66.

11. Mikeal Parsons, *The Departure of Jesus in Luke-Acts. The Ascension Narratives in Context*, JSNTSS 21 (Great Britain: Sheffield Academic Press, 1987).

12. A few other genres have also been suggested: "aretalogy," M. Hadas and M. Smith, *Heroes and Gods*: *Spiritual Biographies in Antiquity* (London: Routledge and Kegan Paul, 1965); "false history," E. Gabba, "True History and False History in Antiquity," *JRS* 71 (1981): 50–62; "folk epic," James M. Dawsey, "Characteristics of Folk-Epic in Acts," in *SBL 1989 Seminar Papers*, ed. by D. Lull, 317–25 (Atlanta: Scholars Press, 1989).

13. David E. Aune, *The New Testament in Its Literary Environment*. LEC (Philadelphia: Westminster Press, 1987). See also Colin Hemer, *The Book of Acts in the Setting of Hellenistic*

History (Tübingen: J. C. B. Mohr, 1989); W. C. van Unnik, "Luke's Second Book and the Rules of Hellenistic Historiography," in *Les Actes des Apôtres: Traditions, rédaction, théologie*, ed. by J. Kremer, 37–60, BETL 48 (Gembloux, Belgium: Duculot, 1979).

14. Hans Conzelmann, *Acts of the Apostles*, Herm (Philadelphia: Fortress Press, 1979); Martin Hengel, *Acts and the History of Earliest Christianity* (Philadelphia: Fortress Press, 1979).

15. Gregory E. Sterling, "Luke-Acts and Apologetic Historiography," in *SBL 1989 Seminar Papers*, ed. by Lull, 326–342.

16. Charles H. Talbert, *What Is A Gospel? The Genre of the Canonical Gospels* (Philadelphia: Fortress Press, 1977); cf. idem, *Literary Patterns*. See also David L. Barr and Judith L. Wentling, "The Conventions of Classical Biography and the Genre of Luke-Acts," in *Luke-Acts: New Perspectives from the Society of Biblical Literature*, ed. by C. Talbert, 63–88 (New York: Crossroad, 1984).

17. Richard I. Pervo, *Profit With Delight. The Literary Genre of the Acts of the Apostles* (Philadelphia: Fortress Press, 1987). See also S. P. and M. J. Schiering, "The Influence of the Ancient Romances on the Acts of the Apostles," *CB* 54 (1978): 81–88.

18. Richard I. Pervo, "Must Luke and Acts Belong to the Same Genre?" in *SBL 1989 Seminar Papers*, ed. by Lull, 309–316.

19. Susan Marie Praeder has argued that Luke-Acts, together, can be read as an ancient novel. See "Luke-Acts and the Ancient Novel," in *SBL 1981 Seminar Papers*, ed. by K. Richards, 269–92 (Chico, CA: Scholars Press, 1981).

20. Gerhard Schneider lists four considerations significant to discussion of Luke's purpose: aims stated in the preface, details in the work that clarify these aims, major themes discussed in the work, and literary genre. Robert Maddox adds three more: the inter-relationship of Luke's two volumes, their date of composition, and the needs of the audience addressed in them. Schneider, "Der Zweck des lukanischen Doppelwerks," *BZ* 21 (1977): 47. Maddox, *The Purpose of Luke-Acts*, SNTW (Edinburgh: T & T Clark, 1985; original, 1982), 20.

21. Cf. Robert F. O'Toole, "Why did Luke Write Acts (Lk-Acts)?" *BTB* 7 (1977): 66–76.

22. Gasque, *History*, 308.

23. For a select bibliography and discussion of Baur's works, see Gasque, *History*; Ernst Haenchen, *The Acts of the Apostles. A Commentary*, 14th ed. (Philadelphia: Westminster Press, 1971; German original, 1965), 15–24; Horton Harris, *The Tübingen School. A Historical and Theological Investigation of the School of F.C. Baur* (Grand Rapids, MI: Baker, 1990; original, 1975). Well-known students of the Tübingen school include David Fredrich Strauss and Albrecht Ritschl.

24. Paul J. Achtemeier, *The Quest for Unity in the New Testament Church: A Study in Paul and Acts* (Philadelphia: Fortress Press, 1987).

25. Charles Talbert, *Luke and the Gnostics: An Examination of the Lucan Purpose* (Nashville: Abingdon Press, 1966). See also Günter Klein, *Die Zwölf Apostel: Ursprung und Gehalt einer Idee*, FRLANT 59 (Göttingen: Vandenhoeck & Ruprecht, 1961).

26. Jack T. Sanders, *The Jews in Luke-Acts* (Philadelphia: Fortress Press, 1987).

27. B. S. Easton, "The Purpose of Acts," in *Early Christianity: the Purpose of Acts, and Other Papers*, ed. by F. C. Grant, 31–118 (Greenwich, CT: Seabury Press, 1954); Haenchen, *Acts*. Another version of the "apologetic purpose" theory holds that Acts was actually written to serve as a defense at Paul's trial in Rome. See the series of articles by A. J. Mattill listed in the bibliography for Schneider, "Zweck."

28. C. K. Barrett, *Luke the Historian in Recent Study* (London: Epworth Press, 1961), 63.

29. Paul Walaskay, *And So We Came to Rome: The Political Perspective of St. Luke* (Cambridge: Cambridge University Press, 1983).

30. Robert L. Brawley, *Luke-Acts and the Jews: Conflict, Apology, and Conciliation*, SBLMS 33 (Atlanta: Scholars Press, 1987); idem, "Paul in Acts: Lucan Apology and Conciliation," in *Luke-Acts*, ed. by Talbert, 129–47.

31. Jacob Jervell, *Luke and the People of God*, 153–207 (Minneapolis, Augsburg, 1972).

32. Nils Dahl, "The Purpose of Luke-Acts," in *Jesus in the Memory of the Early Church*, 87–98 (Minneapolis: Augsburg, 1976).

33. Bruce, *Book of Acts*. J. C. O'Neill, *The Theology of Acts in Its Historical Setting* (London: SPCK, 1961).

34. David Seccombe, *Possessions and the Poor in Luke-Acts*, SNTSU (Linz, 1982).

35. See Maddox, *Purpose*, 13–14; Paul Minear, "Dear Theo: The Kerygmatic Intention and Claim of the Book of Acts," *Int* 27 (1973), 131–50.

36. W. C. van Unnik, "The 'Book of Acts' the Confirmation of the Gospel," *NovT* 4 (1960): 26–59.

37. Maddox, *Purpose*.

38. Philip Esler, *Community and Gospel in Luke-Acts* (Cambridge: Cambridge University Press, 1987).

39. Robert Karris, "Missionary Communities: A New Paradigm for the Study of Luke-Acts," *CBQ* 41 (1979), 80–97.

40. Hans Conzelmann, *The Theology of St. Luke*, 2nd ed. (Philadelphia: Fortress Press, 1982; German original, 1957).

41. "One conclusion that unites nearly all recent study on Luke-Acts is that Conzelmann's classic formulation of the purpose of the Lukan writings . . . was incorrect." W. Ward Gasque, "A Fruitful Field: Recent Study of the Acts of the Apostles," *Int* 42 (1988): 117–31.

42. Ernst Käsemann: "You do not write the history of the Church if you are expecting the end of the world to come any day." See "The Problem of the Historical Jesus," in *Essays on New Testament Themes*, 15–47 (Philadelphia: Fortress Press, 1982; German original, 1954), 28.

43. I. H. Marshall, *Luke: Historian and Theologian* (Grand Rapids: Zondervan, 1970).

44. Paul Schubert, "The Structure and Significance of Luke 24," in *Neutestamentliche Studien für Rudolph Bultmann*, ed. by W. Eltester, 165–86 (Berlin: Topelmann, 1954).

45. Karris, "Communities." But Karris ultimately stresses Luke's pastoral intentions over theological ones.

46. Gasque, *History*, 309.

47. Hemer, *Book of Acts*, 34.

48. William H. Willimon, *The Acts of the Apostles*, IC (Atlanta: John Knox Press, 1988), 11.

49. Ibid.

2. The Composition of Acts

1. In some literature, this is also referred to as the "Egyptian" text type.

2. Haenchen, *Acts*, 50–60.

3. Eldon Jay Epp, *The Theological Tendency of Codex Bezae Cantabrigiensis in Acts* (Cambridge: Cambridge University Press, 1966).

4. Friedrich Blass, "Die zweifache Textüberlieferung in der Apostelgeschichte," *ThStK* 67 (1984): 86–119; Theodore Zahn, *Die Urausgabe der Apostelgeschichte des Lucas*, FGnKaL 9 (Leipzig: Deichert, 1916), 1–10.

5. Martin Dibelius, "The Text of Acts: An Urgent Critical Task," in *Studies in the Acts of the Apostles*, ed. by H. Greeven, 84–92 (New York: Charles Scribner's Sons, 1956; German original, 1941).

6. Material containing so-called "Semitisms" has attracted much attention in this regard; see Max Wilcox, *The Semitisms of Acts* (Oxford: Clarendon Press, 1965), which is discussed briefly in the section on "Sources" in this chapter.

7. A. F. J. Klijn, "In Search of the Original Text of Acts," in *Studies in Luke-Acts*, ed. by L. Keck and J. Martyn, 103–10, esp. 104; (Philadelphia: Fortress Press, 1980; original, 1966); R. Sheldon Mackenzie, "The Western Text of Acts: Some Lucanisms in Selected Sermons," *JBL* 104 (1985): 637–50; Robert F. Hull, "'Lucanisms' in the Western Text of Acts? A Reappraisal," *JBL* 107 (1988): 695–707.

8. Bruce M. Metzger, *A Textual Commentary on the Greek New Testament* (London: United Bible Societies, 1971).

9. W. K. Hobart, *The Medical Language of St. Luke* (Grand Rapids: Baker Books, 1954; original, 1882).

10. Cadbury, *Making*, 219–20.

11. Studies on particular stylistic features of Acts include Henry J. Cadbury, "Four Features of Lucan Style," in *Studies*, ed. by Keck and Martyn, 87–102; James Dawsey, "Literary Unity." Dawsey emphasizes stylistic differences between Acts and the gospel.

12. Cadbury, *Making*, 221–25. Cadbury draws heavily from J.

H. Moulton, *A Grammar of New Testament Greek*, vol. 2 (Edinburgh: T & T Clark, 1920). See also H. F. D. Sparks, "The Semitisms of the Acts," *JTS* n. s. 1 (1950): 16–28.

13. Haenchen, *Acts*, 75.

14. Cadbury, however, warns against excess in assessing Luke's literary skills: "Modern writers are wont to lay more artistic purpose to his credit than the unadorned simplicity of his style warrants." *Making*, 235.

15. Space does not permit discussion of studies on the structure of individual passages. See, e.g., Benjamin J. Hubbard, "The Role of Commissioning Accounts in Acts," in *Perspectives on Luke-Acts*, ed. by Charles Talbert, 187–98 (Danville, VA: Association of Baptist Professors of Religion, 1978); David A. Miesner, "The Missionary Journeys Narrative: Patterns and Implications," in the same volume, 199–214.

16. O'Neill, *Theology*. O'Neill's construction is largely based on that of Phillipe Henri Menoud, "Le Plan des Actes des Apôtres." *NTS* 1 (1954): 44–51.

17. Talbert, *Literary Patterns*. Cf. Morgenthaler, *Die lukanische Geschichtsschreibung*; Praeder, "Parallelisms."

18. M. D. Goulder, *Type and History in Acts* (London: SPCK, 1964). The typological method Goulder uses was developed by Austin Farrer, *St. Matthew and St. Luke* (London: Dacre, 1954).

19. J. L. Houlden, "Review of *Type and History in Acts* by M. D. Goulder," *JTS* 17 (1966): 143–45. Charles Talbert reviews Goulder's work in *RevExp* 63 (1966): 101–03.

20. Haenchen, *Acts*, 86.

21. For a survey, see Jacques Dupont, *The Sources of Acts*: *The Present Position* (London: Darton, Longman, & Todd, 1964).

22. An example of such a study is Karl Löning's *Die Saulustradition in der Apostelgeschichte* (Munich: Aschendorff, 1978). Cf. the objections of Beverly Roberts Gaventa in "Toward a Theology of Acts: Reading and Rereading," *Int* 42 (1988): 146–57.

23. Charles Cutler Torrey, *The Composition and Date of Acts*, HTS 1 (Cambridge: Harvard University Press, 1916).

24. Wilcox, *Semitisms*. Cf. R. A. Martin, "Syntactical Evidence of Aramaic Sources in Acts I-XV, *NTS* 11 (1964–65): 38–59.

25. Cf. Matthew Black, *An Aramaic Approach to the Gospels*

and Acts, 3rd ed. (Oxford: Clarendon Press, 1967). Bruce Metzger cites research to indicate that, overall, the Western text is no more Semitic than the Alexandrian (*Textual Commentary*, 269). But he agrees with Wilcox that an "eclectic approach" should be followed with regard to individual passages.

26. Fred Horton, "Reflections on the Semitisms of Luke-Acts," in *Perspectives*, ed. by Talbert, 1–23.

27. Cf. Matthew Black, "Second Thoughts IX: The Semitic Element in the New Testament," *ExpT* 77 (1965): 20–23.

28. Adolf Harnack, *The Acts of the Apostles*. NTS 3 (London: Williams & Norgate, 1909).

29. Dupont, *Sources*, 62–72.

30. Martin Dibelius "Style Criticism of the Book of Acts," in *Studies*, 1–25 (German original, 1923); "The Acts of the Apostles in the Setting of the History of Early Christian Literature," in *Studies*, 92–206 (German original, 1951). Cf. Etienne Trocmé, *Le "Livre des Actes" et l'Histoire*, Ehpr 45 (Paris: Presses Universitaires de France, 1957); Dupont, *Sources*.

31. Dibelius, "Setting," 199.

32. Werner Georg Kümmel, *Introduction to the New Testament*, 17th ed. (Nashville: Abingdon Press, 1975), 178.

33. Arthur Darby Nock, "The Book of Acts," in *Essays on Religion and the Ancient World*, ed. by Z. Stewart, 2:821–32 (Cambridge: Harvard University Press, 1972).

34. Marcel Dumais, *Le langage de l'évangélisation: L'annonce missionaire en milieu juif (Acts 13:16–41)* (Tourani: Desclée, 1976); Klaus Kliesch, *Das heilsgeschitliche Credo in den Reden der Apostelgeschichte*, BbB 44 (Cologne-Bonn: Peter Hanstein, 1975); Ulich Wilckens, *Die Missionsreden der Apostelgeschichte: Form- und traditionsgeschichtliche Untersuchungen*, 3rd ed., WMANT 5 (Neukirchen-Vluyn: Neukirchener Verlag, 1974).

35. Richard F. Zehnle, *Peter's Pentecost Discourse: Tradition and Lukan Reinterpretation in Peter's Speeches in Acts 2 and 3*, SBLMS 15 (Nashville: Abingdon Press, 1971).

36. Hans Conzelmann, "The Address of Paul on the Areopagus," in *Studies*, ed. by Keck and Martyn, 217–32; Martin Dibelius, "Paul on the Areopagus," in *Studies*, 26–77 (German

original, 1939); idem, "Paul in Athens," in *Studies*, 78–84 (German original, 1939); Bertil Gärtner, *The Areopagus Speech and Natural Revelation*, ASNU 21 (Lund: C. W. K. Gleerup, 1955); V. Gatti, *Il discorso di Paulo ad Atene*: *storia dell'interpretazione essegesiteologia della missione e della religion* (Parma: PVG, 1979); Dean Zweck, "The *Exordium* of the Areopagus Speech, Acts 17:22–23," *NTS* 35 (1989): 94–103.

37. Jerome Neyrey, "The Forensic Defense Speech and Paul's Trial Speeches in Acts 22–26: Form and Function," in *Luke-Acts*, ed. by Talbert, 210–24; Robert F. O'Toole, *Acts 26: The Christological Climax of Paul's Defense (Ac 22:1–26:32)* Anbib 78 (Rome: Biblical Institute, 1978); Fred Veltman, "The Defense Speeches of Paul in Acts," in *Perspectives*, ed. by Talbert, 243–56.

38. Jan Lambrecht, "Paul's Farewell Address at Miletus (Acts 20, 17–38)," in *Les Actes*, ed. by Kremer, 307–37; Hans Joachim Michel, *Die Abschiedsrede des Paulus an die Kirche Apg 20, 17–38: Motivgeschichte und theologische Bedeutung*, SANT 35 (Munich: Kösel-Verlag, 1973); Franz Prast, *Presbyter und Evangelium in nachapostolischer Zeit: Die Abschiedsrede des Paulus in Milet (Apg 20, 17–38) im Rahmen der lukanischen Konzeption der Evangeliumsverkündigung*, FzB 29 (Stuttgart: Verlag Katholisches Bibelwerk, 1979).

39. John Kilgallen, *The Stephen Speech: A Literary and Redactional Study of Acts 7:2–53*, Anbib 67 (Rome: Biblical Institute, 1975); Earl Richard, *Acts 6:1—8:4: The Author's Method of Composition*, SBLDS 41 (Missoula, MT: Scholars Press, 1978).

40. C. H. Dodd, *The Apostolic Preaching and Its Developments* (London: Hodder & Stoughton, 1936).

41. Martin Dibelius, "The Speeches in Acts and Ancient Historiography," in *Studies*, 138–91 (German original, 1949). Also, Eduard Schweizer, "Concerning the Speeches in Acts," in *Studies*, ed. by Keck and Martyn, 208–16.

42. Philipp Vielhauer, "On the 'Paulinism' of Acts," in *Studies*, ed. by Keck and Martyn, 33–50.

43. F. F. Bruce, "The Speeches of Acts—Thirty Years Later," in *Reconciliation and Hope*, ed. by R. Banks, 53–68 (Grand Rapids: Eerdmans, 1974); W. Ward Gasque, "The Speeches in Acts:

Dibelius Reconsidered," in *New Directions in New Testament Studies*, ed. by R. Longenecker and M. C. Tenney, 232–50 (Grand Rapids: Zondervan, 1974).

44. Gerhard Krodel, *Acts*, ACNT (Minneapolis: Augsburg, 1986), 35.

45. F. F. Bruce, "The Acts of the Apostles: Historical Record or Theological Reconstruction?," in *Aufstieg und Niedergang der Römischen Welt: Geschichte und Kultur Roms im Spiegel der neueren Forschung* 11/25, ed. by W. Haase, 2570–603, esp. 2582 (Berlin: Walter de Gruyter, 1985).

46. For a contrary view, see Stanley E. Porter, "Thucydides 1.22.1 and Speeches in Acts: Is There a Thucydidean View?," *NovT* 32 (1990): 121–42.

47. Probably as early as the year 200. See Joseph A. Fitzmyer, "The Authorship of Luke-Acts Reconsidered," in *Luke the Theologian: Aspects of His Teaching*, 1–26, esp. 7–11 (New York: Paulist Press, 1989).

48. Henry J. Cadbury, *Style and Literary Method of Luke*. HTS 6 (Cambridge: Harvard University Press, 1920), 39–72.

49. This assertion is made numerous times throughout the essays collected in *Studies in the Book of Acts*. See, e.g., 97, n. 4.

50. Dupont, *Sources*, 75–93, 122–31.

51. Ibid.

52. Jürgen Wehnert, *Die Wir-Passagagen der Apostelgeschichte: Ein lukanisches Stilmittel aus jüdischer Tradition*, (Göttingen: Vandenhoeck & Ruprecht, 1989).

53. Vernon K. Robbins, "The We-Passages in Acts and Ancient Sea Voyages," *BR* 20 (1975): 5–18; "By Land and By Sea: The We-Passages and Ancient Sea Voyages," in *Perspectives*, ed. by Talbert, 215–42. See also Susan Marie Praeder, "Acts 27:1—28:16: Sea Voyages in Ancient Literature and the Theology of Luke-Acts," *CBQ* 46 (1984): 683–706.

54. Fitzmyer, "Authorship," 16–22. Also William S. Kurz, "Narrative Approaches to Luke-Acts," *Biblica* 68 (1987): 195–220, esp. 116–220; Wehnert, *Wir Passagen*.

55. Haenchen, *Acts*, 112–16.

56. Morton S. Enslin contests this point. See *Reapproaching Paul* (Philadelphia: Westminster Press, 1962); "Luke the Literary

Physician," in *Studies in New Testament and Early Christian Literature*: *Essays in Honor of Allen P. Wikgren*, NovTSup 33, ed. by D. Aune, 135–43 (Leiden: Brill, 1972).

57. Vielhauer, "Paulinism."

58. Haenchen, *Acts*, 48.

59. Gasque, *History*, 287.

60. Fitzmyer, "Authorship," 3–7, 11–16.

61. Hemer, *Book of Acts*, 365–410; J. A. T. Robinson, *Redating the New Testament* (London: Westminster Press, 1976). Cf. Adolf Harnack, *The Date of the Acts and of the Synoptic Gospels*, NTS 4 (New York: Putnam, 1911), 93–99.

62. C. S. C. Williams believes Acts was written before the gospel received its final form and may therefore be dated between 66–70. See "The Date of Luke-Acts," *ExpT* 64 (1952–53): 283–84.

63. Conzelmann, *Acts*, xxvii–xxxiii; Haenchen, *Acts* 1–14.

64. John T. Townsend, "The Date of Luke-Acts," in *Luke-Acts*, ed. by Talbert, 47–62; O'Neill, *Theology*, 1–28.

65. Emanuel Hirsh, "Die drei Berichte der Apostelgeschichte über die Bekehrung des Paulus," *ZNW* 28 (1929): 305–12.

66. Ernst von Dobschütz, "Die Berichte über die Bekehrung des Paulus," *ZNW* 29 (1930): 144–47; Cadbury, "Four Features."

3. The Theology of Acts: God, Jesus, and the Holy Spirit

1. For a study that makes an attempt, see Francois Bovon, "Le Dieu de Luc," *RSR* 69 (1981): 279–300.

2. J. G. C. Anderson, "Paganism and Christianity in the Upper Tembris Valley," in *Studies in the History and Art of the Eastern Provinces of the Roman Empire*, ed. by W. Ramsay, 183–227 (Aberdeen: Aberdeen University Press, 1906), esp. 211; Bruce, *Acts*, 333.

3. See Paul Trebilco, "Paul and Silas—'Servants of the Most High God' (Acts 16:16–18)," *JSNT* 36 (1989): 51–73.

4. O'Toole, *Unity*, 23–32. See also Earl Richard, "The Divine Purpose: The Jews and the Gentile Mission," in *Luke-Acts*, ed. by Talbert, 188–209.

5. O'Toole, *Unity*, 27–28; John Navone, *Themes of St. Luke* (Rome: Gregorian University Press, 1970), 100–102; Walter Grundmann, "*dei, deon, esti*," in *TDNT* 2:21–25.

6. Conzelmann, *Theology*, 137–234.

7. Karris, "Communities," Werner G. Kümmel, "Current Theological Accusations Against Luke," *ANQ* 16 (1975): 131–45 (French original, 1970).

8. Studies on this motif have been offered by Henry J. Cadbury, Nils A. Dahl, William Kurz, Eduard Lohse and Paul Schubert. For summary and critique, see Charles H. Talbert, "Promise and Fulfillment in Lucan Theology," in *Luke-Acts*, ed. by Talbert, 91–103; Darrell L. Bock, *Proclamation from Prophecy and Pattern: Lucan Old Testament Christology*, JSNTSS 12 (Great Britain: Sheffield Academic Press, 1987), 27–37.

9. Martin Rese, *Alttestamentliche Motive in der Christologie des Lukas*, SZNT 1 (Gütersloh: Gütersloher Verlagshaus Gerd Mohn, 1969).

10. Eric Franklin, *Christ the Lord: A Study in the Purpose and Theology of Luke-Acts* (Philadelphia: Westminster Press, 1975); Bock, *Proclamation*.

11. Robert J. Karris, *What Are They Saying About Luke and Acts? A Theology of the Faithful God* (New York: Paulist Press, 1979); idem, "Communities."

12. Karris, "Communities," 93.

13. Francois Bovon, *Luke the Theologian: Thirty-three Years of Research, (1950-1983)* (Allison Park, PA: Pickwick Publications, 1987), 120.

14. Ibid., 177–97.

15. Emmeram Kränkl, *Jesus der Knecht Gottes: Die heilsgeschichtliche Stellung Jesu in den Reden der Apostelgeschichte*, BU 8 (Regensburg: Pustet, 1972).

16. "Benefactor": Frederick W. Danker, *Luke*, 2nd ed., PC (Philadelphia: Fortress Press, 1987); Gerhard Krodel, *Acts*, PC (Philadelphia: Fortress Press, 1981). "Immortal": Charles H. Talbert, "The Concept of Immortals in Mediterranean Antiquity," *JBL* (1975): 419–36. "Philosopher": Talbert, *Literary Patterns*; idem, *What Is A Gospel?*. "Prophet": Paul Minear, *To Heal and to Reveal: The Prophetic Vocation According to Luke* (New York: Seabury Press, 1976). For summary of the first three models, see Powell, *What Are They Saying About Luke?*, 63–66.

17. See summary in Bovon, *Luke the Theologian*, 135–43.

18. John A. T. Robinson, "The Most Primitive Christology of All?" in *Twelve New Testament Studies*, 139–53 (London: SCM Press, 1962; original, 1956).

19. C. F. D. Moule, "The Christology of Acts," in *Studies*, ed. by Keck and Martyn, 159–85; Gerhard Lohfink, "Christologie und Gesichtsbild in Apg 3, 19–21," *BZ* 13 (1969): 223–41; Donald L. Jones, "The Title *Christos* in Luke-Acts," *CBQ* 32 (1970): 69–76.

20. Robinson, "Primitive"; Ferdinand Hahn, *The Titles of Jesus in Christology: Their History in Early Christianity* (London: Lutterworth, 1969; German original, 1963), 107.

21. Moule, "Christology"; Zehnle, *Pentecost*; Donald L. Jones, "The Title *Kyrios* in Luke-Acts," in *SBL 1974 Seminar Papers*, 2 vols, ed. by G. MacRae, 2:85–101 (Cambridge: Society of Biblical Literature, 1974).

22. Moule, "Christology," 160–66.

23. Bock, *Proclamation*.

24. Donald L. Jones, "The Title *Huois Theou* in Acts," in *SBL 1985 Seminar Papers*, ed. by K. Richards, 451–63 (Atlanta: Society of Biblical Literature, 1985); "The Title 'Servant' in Luke-Acts," in *Luke-Acts*, ed. by Talbert, 148–65; "Title *Christos*"; "Title *Kyrios*."

25. Conzelmann, *Theology*, 185–87; 207–09.

26. Moule, "Christology," 179–80.

27. George W. MacRae, "'Whom Heaven Must Receive Until the Time': Reflections on the Christology of Acts," *Int* 27 (1973): 151–65. The first and third modes of presence listed by MacRae are noted also by Conzelmann, *Theology*, 185–87.

28. Gerhard Krodel, *Acts* (PC), 4–5; *Acts* (ACNT), 54, 175. See also, Marshall, *Historian and Theologian*, 157, 179–82.

29. Conzelmann, *Theology*, 202–06.

30. Gerhard Lohfink, *Die Himmelfahrt Jesu: Untersuchungen zu den Himmelfahrts-und Erhöhungstexten bei Lukas*, SANT 26 (Munich: Kösel-Verlag, 1971). See also Mikeal C. Parsons, *The Departure of Jesus in Luke-Acts: The Ascension Narratives in Context*, JSNTSS 21 (Sheffield: JSOT Press, 1987).

31. Eric Franklin, *Christ the Lord*, 29–47; See also Helmut

Flender, *St. Luke: Theologian of Redemptive History* (Philadelphia: Fortress Press, 1967; German original, 1965); Kränkl, *Knecht Gottes*, 176–86.

32. Maddox, *Purpose*, 139.

33. Luke 1:47, 69, 71, 77; 2:11, 30; 3:6; 19:9; Acts 4:12, 5:31; 7:25; 13:23, 26, 47; 16:17; 27:34; 28:28.

34. See Werner Foerster, *"sōzō and sōtēria* in the Greek World," and Georg Fohrer," *sōzō* and *sōtēria* in the Old Testament," in *TDNT* 7:966–80.

35. Danker, *Luke*, 28–46, 82–99.

36. Talbert, "Concept of Immortals."

37. Gerhard Voss, *Die Christologie der lukanischen Schriften in Grundzügen*, SN 2 (Brügge: Desclée de Brouwer, 1965), 45–60.

38. Minear, *Heal and Reveal*, 102–11. Danker has described Jesus in Luke as a prophet like Elijah (*Luke*, 67–71).

39. Marshall, *Historian and Theologian*, 77–102, 157–95.

40. Kränkl emphasizes the ascension over the resurrection as the decisive moment in salvation history: forgiveness of sins and the gift of the Spirit are benefits of the ascension (*Knecht Gottes*, 166–86). Richard Glöckner attempts to show that Luke does not isolate any one phase of Jesus' life (death, resurrection, ascension) as salvific, but regards the whole sweep of Jesus' life as redemptive. *Die Verkündigung des Heils beim Evangelisten Lukas*, WS 9 (Mainz: Matthias Grünewald Verlag, 1976).

41. See also Beverly Roberts Gaventa, *From Darkness to Light: Aspects of Conversion in the New Testament*, OBT (Philadelphia: Fortress Press, 1986), 52–129; Jacques Dupont, "Conversion in the Acts of the Apostles," in *The Salvation of the Gentiles: Essays on the Acts of the Apostles*, 61–84 (New York: Paulist Press, 1979; French original, 1968).

42. Arnold Ehrhardt, "The Construction and Purpose of the Acts of the Apostles," in *ST* 12 (1958): 45–79, esp. 67.

43. Heinrich von Baer, *Der Heilige Geist in den Lukasschriften*, BWANT 3/3 (Stuttgart: W. Kohlhammer, 1926). Cf. Augustin George, "L'Espirit-Saint dans l'oeuvre de Luc," *RevisitB* 85 (1978): 500–42.

44. F. F. Bruce, "The Holy Spirit in the Acts of the Apostles," *Int* 27 (1973): 166–83, esp. 170–71; A. T. Lincoln, "Theology and

History in the Interpretation of Luke's Pentecost," *ExpT* 96 (1985): 204–09, esp. 206.

45. Jacques Dupont, "The First Christian Pentecost," in *Salvation*, 35–60 (originally published, 1963); Jacob Kremer, *Pfingstbericht und Pfingstgeschehen*: *Eine exegetische Untersuchung zu Apg 2, 1–13*, SB 63/64 (Stuttgart: Verlag Katholisches Bibelwerk, 1973), 11–27.

46. Eduard Lohse, *"pentēcostē,"* in *TDNT* 6:44–53.

47. Jacob Jervell, "Sons of the Prophets: The Holy Spirit in the Acts of the Apostles," in *The Unknown Paul: Essays on Luke-Acts and Early Christian History*, 96–121 (Minneapolis: Augsburg, 1984).

48. Alexander R. Vidler, *Christian Belief* (London: SCM Press, 1950), 61–62.

49. Eduard Schweizer, *"pneuma, pneumatikos, pneō, empneō, pnoē ekveō, theoneustos*: The New Testament," in *TDNT* 6:396–455, esp. 406, n. 474.

50. Ibid., 404–06.

51. Roger Stronstad, *The Charismatic Theology of St. Luke* (Peabody, MA: Hendrickson, 1984), 13–27, 75–82. See also G. W. H. Lampe, "The Holy Spirit in the Writings of St. Luke," in *Studies in the Gospels: Essays in Memory of R. H. Lightfoot*, ed. by D. E. Nineham, 159–200 (Oxford: Basil Blackwell, 1955); M. A. Chevallier, "Luc et l'Espirit saint. A la memoire du P. Augustin George (1951–1977)," *RevScRel* 56 (1982): 1–16.

52. Bovon, *Luke the Theologian*, 219.

53. John H. E. Hull, *The Holy Spirit in the Acts of the Apostles* (Cleveland: World, 1968), 174.

54. Lampe, "Holy Spirit," 163.

55. Bruce, "Holy Spirit," 172–74.

56. Bruce, "Holy Spirit," 178; Marshall, *Historian and Theologian*, 199–202; Schweizer, *"pneuma,"* 407–13. Hull thinks the Spirit does work to sanctify believers and create community in Acts (*Holy Spirit*, 43–46).

57. On the connection of Spirit and church, see also G. Haya-Prats, *L'Esprit force de l'église: Sa nature et son activité d'après les Actes des Apôtres* (Paris: Cerf, 1975); K. Stalder, "Der Heilige Geist in der lukanischen Ekkesiologie," *US* 30 (1975): 287–93. On

the theme of mission or witness in Acts, see Howard Clark Kee, *Good News to the Ends of the Earth*: *The Theology of Acts* (Philadelphia: Trinity Press International, 1990); Robert L. Maddox, *Witnesses to the Ends of the Earth*: *The Pattern of Mission in the Book of Acts* (Enfield, Australia: United Theological College, 1980); Allison Trites, *The New Testament Concept of Witness* (Cambridge: Cambridge University Press, 1977), 128–53.

58. Leo O'Reilly, *Word and Sign in the Acts of the Apostles*: *A Study in Lucan Theology*, AG 82 (Rome: Editrice Pontificia Universita Gregoriana, 1987).

59. For this reason Schweizer thinks the Spirit should not be credited with the miracles *"pneuma,"* 407.

60. Jervell, "Sons of Prophets." Also Chevalier, "Luc et l'Espirit."

61. See also Bruce, "Holy Spirit," 180–83.

62. Ibid., 177–78.

63. Canon J. Giblet, "Baptism in the Spirit in the Acts of the Apostles," *OIC* 10 (1974): 162–71. Hull thinks repentance, faith, and willingness to be baptized are normative (*Holy Spirit*, 99, 119–20).

64. Michael Quesnel, *Baptisés dans L'Espirit*: *Baptême et Espirit Saint dans les Actes des Apôtres*, LD 120 (Paris: Cerf, 1985).

65. Lampe, "Holy Spirit," 168–70. Cf. Schweizer, *"pneuma,"* 414.

66. Ernst Käsemann, "Ministry and Community in the New Testament," in *Essays on New Testament Themes*, 63–94, esp. 89–91, German original, 1949); "The Disciples of John the Baptist in Ephesus," in the same volume, 136–48 (German original, 1952). Cf. Nikolaus Alder, *Taufe und Handauflegung. Eine exegetische-theologische Untersuchung von Apg, 8, 14–17*, NTAbh 19:3 (Münster: Aschendorff, 1951).

67. Bovon, *Luke the Theologian*, 219.

68. C. K. Barrett, "Light on the Holy Spirit from Simon Magus (Acts 8, 4–25)," in *Les Actes*, ed. by Kremer, 281–95. Cf. Victor E. Pfitzner, "Pneumatic Apostleship?," in *Wort in der Zeit*: *Festgabe für Karl Heinrich Rengstorff zum 75 Geburstag*, ed. by W. Haubeck and M. Bachmann, 210–35 (Leiden: E. J. Brill, 1980).

69. James D. G. Dunn, *Baptism in the Holy Spirit: A Reexamination of the New Testament Teaching on the Gift of the Spirit in Relation to Pentecostalism Today*, SBT (Naperville, IL: Alec R. Allenson, 1970), esp. 55–68.

70. Marshall, *Historian and Theologian*, 169–70, 188–202. Cf. Stalder, "Heilige Geist."

71. Beverly Roberts Gaventa, "Toward a Theology of Acts: Reading and Rereading," *Int* 42 (1988): 146–57.

72. Gaventa's concern is that they do not take seriously the character of Acts as narrative (Ibid., 149), a matter to which we shall attend in chapter 6 of this book.

4. The Church in Acts: Eschatology and Ecclesiology

1. For additional summaries of these views see John T. Carroll, *Response to the End of History: Eschatology and Situation in Luke-Acts*, SBLDS 92 (Atlanta: Scholars Press, 1988), 1–30; Bovon, *Luke the Theologian*, 1–77; Powell, *What Are They Saying About Luke?*, 42–45, 76–79.

2. Conzelmann, *Theology*.

3. Conzelmann believes that in Acts the theme of the delay of the parousia is "not so much developed as presupposed." *Acts*, xiv.

4. Also, Vielhauer (discussed in this book, pp. 35–36, 91–94) and Borgen, Kaestli, Zmijewski, Robinson, and Braumann, all discussed in Carroll, *Response*, 6–9.

5. A. J. Mattill, *Luke and the Last Things: A Perspective for the Understanding of Lukan Thought* (Dillsboro, NC: Western North Carolina Press, 1979). See also Fred O. Francis, "Eschatology and History in Luke-Acts," *JAAR* 37 (1969): 49–63.

6. Robert H. Smith, "The Eschatology of Acts and Contemporary Exegesis," *CTM* 29 (1958): 641–63; "History and Eschatology in Luke-Acts," *CTM* 29 (1958): 881–901. Richard H. Hiers, "The Problem of the Delay of the Parousia in Luke-Acts," *NTS* 20 (1974): 145–55.

7. Carroll, *Response*.

8. Flender, *Redemptive History*.

9. Franklin, *Christ the Lord*.

10. Maddox, *Purpose*.

11. J. Bradley Chance, *Jerusalem, the Temple, and the New Age in Luke-Acts* (Macon, GA: Mercer University Press, 1988).

12. Hans Bartsch, *Wachet aber zu jeder Zeit! Entwurf einer Auslegung des Lukasevangeliums* (Hamburg-Bergstedt: Herbert Reich-Evangelischer Verlag, 1963).

13. Talbert, *Luke and the Gnostics*.

14. Gaventa, "Eschatology."

15. The strongest proponent of this two-front theory is Stephen G. Wilson, but he holds it only for the gospel, thinking that Acts was written later when all hope of an imminent return was gone. "Lukan Eschatology," *NTS* 15 (1969–70): 330–47. In spite of this, his two-front theory is often applied to both Luke and Acts. See, e.g., H. Farrell, *The Eschatological Perspective of Luke-Acts*, Ph.D. diss., Boston University, 1972.

16. E. Earle Ellis, *Eschatology in Luke*, FB (Philadelphia: Fortress Press, 1972).

17. Easton, "Purpose."

18. Klein, *Zwölf Apostel*.

19. Walter Schmithals, *The Office of Apostle in the Early Church* (Nashville: Abingdon Press, 1969; German original, 1961), 265–77. Schmithals himself finds the origin of the apostolate in Syrian Gnosticism. Cf. Karl Rengstorf's study, which traces the apostolate to an office within Judaism. *"apostellō,"* in *TDNT*, 1:397–448.

20. Jean Danielou, *L'Eglise des apôtres* (Paris: Editions du Seuil, 1970).

21. See J. H. Elliott, "A Catholic Gospel: Reflections on 'Early Catholicism' in the New Testament," *CBQ* 31 (1969): 213–23; Kevin Giles, "Is Luke an Exponent of 'Early Protestantism'?," 2 parts, *EvQ* 54/4 (1982): 193–205 and 55/1 (1983): 3–20; W. G. Kümmel, "Accusations"; I. H. Marshall, "Early Catholicism in the New Testament," in *New Dimensions*, ed. by Longenecker and Tenney, 217–231.

22. Conzelmann, *Acts*; Schmithals, *Office*.

23. Eduard Schweizer, *Church Order in the New Testament*, SBT 32 (London: SCM Press, 1961), 63–76. Also, Marcel Dumais,

"Ministères, Charismes, et Esprit dans l'oeuvve de Luc," *EglTheol* 9 (1978): 413–53.

24. Giles, "Exponent."

25. On the offices, see Giles, "Exponent," part 2; Bovon, *Luke the Theologian*, 359–76.

26. Gasque, "Fruitful Field," 126.

27. E. Rasco, "Spirito e istituzione nell'opera lucana," *RevisitB* 30 (1982): 301–22.

28. Joseph Tyson, "The Emerging Church and the Problem of Authority in Acts," *Int* 42 (1988): 132–45. See also, Tannehill, *Narrative Unity*, vol. 2.

29. Elisabeth Schüssler Fiorenza, *In Memory of Her. A Feminist Theological Reconstruction of Christian Origins* (New York: Crossroad, 1987; original, 1983); Elisabeth Tetlow, *Women and Ministry in the New Testament* (New York: Paulist Press, 1980); see also Powell, *What Are They Saying About Luke?*, 93–97.

30. Haenchen, *Acts*, 48–49.

31. Jerome Kodell, "'The Word of God Grew': The Ecclesial Tendency of *Logos* in Acts 1,7; 12,24; 19,20," *Biblica* 55 (1974): 505–19.

32. Schuyler Brown, *Apostasy and Perseverance in the Theology of Luke*, AnBib 36 (Rome: Biblical Institute, 1969).

33. Jervell, "The Signs of an Apostle: Paul's Miracles," in *Unknown Paul*, 77–95.

34. O'Reilly, *Word and Sign*.

35. Paul Achtemeier, "The Lucan Perspective on the Miracles of Jesus: A Preliminary Sketch," *JBL* 94 (1975): 547–62, esp. 553.

36. G. W. H. Lampe, "Miracles in the Acts of the Apostles," in *Miracles: Cambridge Studies in their Philosophy and History*, ed. by C. F. D. Moule, 163–78 (London: A. R. Mowbray & Co., 1965).

37. On miracles in Acts, see also Augustin George, "Les miracles dans l'oeuvre de Luc," in *Les miracles de Jésus selon le Nouveau Testament*, ed. by X. Léon-Dufour, 249–68 (Paris: Editions de Seuil, 1977); Frans Neirynck, "The Miracle Stories in the Acts of the Apostles," in *Les Actes des Apôtres*, ed. by Kremer, 169–213.

38. Susan R. Garrett, *The Demise of the Devil: Magic and the*

Demonic in Luke's Writings (Minneapolis: Fortress Press, 1989). See also Joseph Fitzmyer, "Satan and Demons in Luke-Acts," in *Luke the Theologian*, 146–74.

39. Käsemann, "Ministry and Community," 92.

40. Ulrich Wilckens, "Interpreting Luke-Acts in a Period of Existentialist Theology," in *Studies*, ed. by Keck and Martyn, 60–83, esp. 67–69; Joseph Fitzmyer, *The Gospel According to Luke*, 2 vols., AB (Garden City: Doubleday & Co., 1981), 1:22–23.

41. C. K. Barrett, "Theologia Crucis—in Acts?," in *Theologia Crucis—Signum Crucis: Festschrift für Erich Dinkler*, ed. by C. Anderson and G. Klein, 73–84 (Tübingen: J. C. B. Mohr, 1979); Gaventa, "Theology."

42. Tannehill, *Narrative Unity*, vol. 2.

43. Jacques Dupont, "The Salvation of the Gentiles," in *Salvation*, 11–34.

44. Stephen G. Wilson, *The Gentiles and the Gentile Mission in Luke-Acts*, SNTSMS 23 (Cambridge: Cambridge University Press, 1973).

45. Haenchen, "Source Material," 278.

46. Augustin George, "Israël dans l'oeuvre de Luc," *RB* 75 (1968): 481–525; Joachim Gnilka, *Die Verstockung Israels: Isaias 6, 9–10 in der Theologie der Synoptiker*, SANT 3 (Munich: Kösel-Verlag, 1961); Maddox, *Purpose*; O'Neill, *Theology*; Sanders, *Jews*; Joseph Tyson, "The Problem of Jewish Rejection in Acts," in *Luke-Acts and Jewish People*, ed. by Tyson, 124–37; Wilson, *Gentiles*.

47. Sanders, *Jews*, 317.

48. Michael J. Cook, "The Mission to the Jews in Luke-Acts: Unraveling Luke's 'Myth of the Myriads'," in *Luke-Acts and Jewish People*, ed. by Tyson, 102–23.

49. Brawley, *Luke-Acts and the Jews*.

50. David L. Tiede, "'Glory to Thy People Israel': Luke-Acts and the Jews," in *Luke-Acts and Jewish People*, ed. by Tyson, 21–34. Cf. Tiede, *Prophecy and History in Luke-Acts* (Philadelphia: Fortress Press, 1980).

51. Chance, *Jerusalem*; Franklin, *Christ the Lord*; Donald Juel, *Luke-Acts: The Promise of History* (Atlanta: John Knox Press, 1983); Mattill, *Last Things*.

52. Jervell, *Luke and People of God*.

53. Joseph Fitzmyer, "The Jewish People and the Mosaic Law in Luke-Acts," in *Luke the Theologian*, 175–202.

54. Jacob Jervell, "The Church of Jews and Godfearers," in *Luke-Acts and Jewish People*, ed. by Tyson, 11–20.

55. Bovon, *Luke the Theologian*, 323.

56. Marilyn Salmon, "Insider or Outsider? Luke's Relationship with Judaism," in *Luke-Acts and Jewish People*, ed. by Tyson, 76–82.

57. Conzelmann, *Acts*, xlvii.

58. Walaskay, *So We Came*, 25.

59. Ibid., 66.

60. Ernst Haenchen, "Judentum und Christentum in der Apostelgeschichte," *ZNW* 54 (1963): 155–87.

61. Walaskay, *So We Came*.

62. Esler, *Community*.

63. Richard J. Cassidy, *Society and Politics in the Acts of the Apostles* (Maryknoll, NY: Orbis Books, 1987).

64. Powell, *What Are They Saying About Luke?*, 111–21.

65. Bovon, *Luke the Theologian*, 377.

66. Giles, "Exponent," part 1, 194–202.

67. Marshall, *Historian and Theologian*, 214.

68. Schweizer, "*pneuma*," 411.

69. G. R. Beasley-Murray, *Baptism in the New Testament* (New York: St. Martin's Press, 1963), 93–122.

70. Giles, "Exponent," part 1, 202–05.

71. James D. G. Dunn, *Unity and Diversity in the New Testament: An Inquiry into the Character of Earliest Christianity* (Philadelphia: Westminster Press, 1977), 163.

72. In addition to those discussed here, see Philippe H. Menoud, "Les Actes des apôtres et l'eucharistie," *RHPR* 33 (1953): 21–35.

73. I. Howard Marshall, *Last Supper and Lord's Supper* (Grand Rapids: Eerdmans, 1980), 126–33.

74. Hans Lietzmann, *Mass and Lord's Supper* (Leiden: E. J. Brill, 1953; German original, 1926), 204–15.

75. For a definitive rebuttal, see Gerard S. Sloyan, "Primitive and 'Pauline' Concepts of the Eucharist," *CBQ* 23 (1961): 1–13. Cf. Marshall, *Last Supper*, 131–33.

76. Joachim Wanke, *Beobachtungen zum Eucharistieverständnis des Lukas auf Grund der lukanischen Mahlberichte* (Leipzig: St. Benno Verlag, 1973).

77. Luke T. Johnson, *Sharing Possessions*: *Mandate and Symbol of Faith* (Philadelphia: Fortress Press, 1981).

78. Walter E. Pilgrim, *Good News to the Poor*: *Wealth and Poverty in Luke-Acts* (Minneapolis: Augsburg, 1981).

5. Reading Acts as History

1. I. H. Marshall, *The Acts of the Apostles*: *An Introduction and Commentary*, TNTC (Grand Rapids: Eerdmans, 1980), 17.

2. Marshall, *Historian and Theologian*.

3. Pervo, *Profit With Delight*.

4. Van Unnik, "Luke's Second Book," 41.

5. Gärtner, *Areopagus Speech*, 7–36.

6. Eckhardt Plümacher, *Lukas als hellenistischer Schriftsteller*: *Studien zur Apostelgeschichte*, SUNT 9 (Göttingen: Vandenhoeck & Ruprecht, 1972).

7. Van Unnik, "Luke's Second Book."

8. Haenchen, "Book of Acts as Source Material."

9. Van Unnik, "Luke's Second Book," 50–51. Cf. Hemer, *Book of Acts*, 63–100.

10. Barrett, *Luke the Historian*, 24–25.

11. Gerd Lüdemann, *Early Christianity according to the Traditions in Acts*: *A Commentary* (Minneapolis: Fortress Press, 1989; German original, 1987).

12. Since Martin Dibelius, "Style Criticism of the Book of Acts," in *Studies*, 1–25 (German original, 1923). But see Gaventa's objections in "Theology."

13. Richard Jeske, "Luke and Paul on the Apostle Paul," *Cur TM* 4 (1977): 28–38, esp. 29.

14. Günther Bornkamm, *Paul* (New York: Harper & Row, 1971; German original, 1969), xxi.

15. Hemer, *Book of Acts*.

16. Adrian N. Sherwin-White, *Roman Society and Roman Law in the New Testament* (Oxford: Clarendon Press, 1963), 189. Cf. F. F. Bruce, "Historical Record," 2576–2577.

17. Gordon Hewart, "Presidential Address," *PCA* 24 (1927): 27. Cf. Bruce, "Historical Record," 2576.

18. Harry W. Tajra, *The Trial of St. Paul: A Juridical Exegesis of the Second Half of the Acts of the Apostles*, WUNT 35 (Tübingen: J. C. B. Mohr, 1989).

19. Hengel, *Acts*, 39.

20. See also Hemer, *Book of Acts*, 101–220.

21. W. Ward Gasque, "The Book of Acts and History," in *Unity and Diversity in New Testament Theology: Essays in Honor of George E. Ladd*, ed. by R. Guelich, 54–72, esp. 55 (Grand Rapids: Eerdmans, 1978).

22. Krodel, *Acts* (PC), 103–04.

23. Bruce, "Historical Record," 2578.

24. Marshall, *Historian and Theologian*, 69.

25. Hans Conzelmann and Andreas Lindemann, *Interpreting the New Testament, An Introduction to the Principles and Methods of New Testament Exegesis* (Peabody, MA: Hendrickson, 1988; German original, 1985), 36.

26. Hans Conzelmann, "Review of W. Ward Gasque, *A History of the Criticism of the Acts of the Apostles*," *Erasmus* 28 (1976): 65–68, esp. 68.

27. Henry J. Cadbury, *The Book of Acts in History* (New York: Harper and Bros., 1955), 120.

28. Krodel, *Acts* (PC), 104–08.

29. Bruce, *Book of Acts*.

30. Lüdemann, *Early Christianity*. Cf. A. J. Mattill, "The Value of Acts as a Source for the Study of Paul," in *Perspectives*, ed. by Talbert, 99–111, esp. 87–95.

31. Haenchen, *Acts*, 107.

32. Bruce, "Historical Record," 2578.

33. See Mattill, "Value of Acts."

34. Lüdemann, *Early Christianity*.

35. But Lüdemann accepts it as historical. Ibid., 240–41.

36. Krodel, *Acts* (PC), 95–102; Achtemeier, *Quest for Unity*.

37. Charles H. Talbert lists seven in "Again: Paul's Visits to Jerusalem," *NovT* (1967): 26–40, esp. 26, n. 3.

38. Hemer, *Book of Acts*, 261–307.

39. Hengel, *Acts*, 117.

40. Bruce, "Historical Record," 2580. He thinks the private meeting referred to in Galatians 2:1–2 probably matches the visit in Acts 11:30 rather than that in Acts 15, but even so Galatians 1:18–20 does not square with Acts 9:26–29.

41. Achtemeier, *Quest for Unity*, 75.

42. Vielhauer, "Paulinism."

43. Albert Schweitzer, *The Mysticism of Paul the Apostle* (New York: Macmillan, 1955; German original, 1930), 6. Cf. Bruce, "Historical Record," 2586.

44. Gärtner, *Areopagus Speech*.

45. Gasque, "Book of Acts," 64; idem, *History*, 288.

46. Bruce, "Historical Record," 2579–2582.

47. Marshall, *Historian and Theologian*, 75.

48. Jervell, *Unknown Paul*, 13–25, 52–95. Hemer likewise considers the preference scholars give to information provided by Paul over that provided in Acts to be based on an unwarranted assumption. *Book of Acts*, 24.

49. Mattill, "Value of Acts."

50. The distinction between the two is stressed by Cadbury, *Acts in History*, 3.

51. See especially Jack Finegan, *The Archaeology of the New Testament: The Mediterranean World of the Early Christian Apostles* (Boulder, CO: Westview, 1981); Edwin Yamauchi, *The Archaeology of the New Testament Cities in Western Asia Minor* (Grand Rapids: Baker, 1980).

52. See especially Wayne A. Meeks, *The First Urban Christians: The Social World of the Apostle Paul* (New Haven: Yale University Press, 1983); John E. Stambaugh and David L. Balch, *The New Testament and Its Social Environment* (Philadelphia: Westminster Press, 1986).

6. Reading Acts as Literature

1. E. J. Goodspeed, *An Introduction to the New Testament* (Chicago: University of Chicago Press, 1937), 187. On Luke's gift for storytelling, see also Geoffrey Nuttal, *The Moment of Recognition: Luke As Story-Teller* (London: Athlone Press, 1978).

2. A notable example is Charles Talbert, who regards the

genre of Luke-Acts as biography, but has contributed vastly to our understanding of its literary motifs.

3. See Mark Allan Powell, *The Bible and Modern Literary Criticism*: *A Critical Assessment and Annotated Bibliography* (Westport, CT: Greenwood Press, 1991).

4. Two other approaches, much applied to the gospels, have been used only slightly so far with Acts: structuralism and reader-response criticism. For an example of the former, see Roland Barthes, "A Structuralist Analysis of a Narrative from Acts X-XI," in *Structuralism and Biblical Hermeneutics*: *A Collection of Essays*, ed. by A. Johnson, 109–43 (Pittsburgh: Pickwick Press, 1979; French original, 1970); of the latter, John Darr, *Character Building*: *The Critic, The Reader, and the Characters of Luke-Acts* (Louisville: Westminster/John Knox, forthcoming); Praeder, "Parallelisms."

5. For application of the method to New Testament studies, see George Kennedy, *New Testament Interpretation Through Rhetorical Criticism* (Chapel Hill: University of North Carolina Press, 1984); Burton Mack, *Rhetoric and the New Testament*, GBS (Minneapolis: Fortress Press, 1989).

6. See esp. Chaim Perelmann and L. Olbrechts-Tyteca, *The New Rhetoric*: *A Treatise on Argumentation* (Notre Dame: Notre Dame University, 1969).

7. Kennedy, *New Testament Interpretation*, 114–40.

8. Aristotle also recognizes "epideictic rhetoric," which seeks to persuade the audience to hold or reaffirm some point of view in the present; its typical features are praise or blame.

9. Mack, *Rhetoric*, 89–92.

10. Dumais, *Lange*.

11. Perelmann and Olbrechts-Tyteca, *New Rhetoric*, 14.

12. Gärtner, *Areopagus Speech*.

13. Neyrey, "Forensic Defense Speech."

14. Robert F. O'Toole, *Acts 26*: *The Christological Climax of Paul's Defense (Ac 22:1—26:32)*, AnBib 78 (Rome: Biblical Institute, 1978).

15. See Mark Allan Powell, *What Is Narrative Criticism?*, GBS (Minneapolis: Fortress Press, 1990). Important secular studies on which the method is based include Wayne C. Booth, *The*

Rhetoric of Fiction, 2nd ed. (Chicago: University of Chicago Press, 1983) and Seymour Chatman, *Story and Discourse: Narrative Structure in Fiction and Film* (Ithaca, NY: Cornell University Press, 1978).

16. On this concept, see Powell, *Narrative Criticism*, 19–20; Chatman, *Story and Discourse*, 147–51.

17. Allen Walworth, *The Narrator of Acts*, Ph.D. diss., Southern Baptist Theological Seminary, 1984.

18. Cf. Tannehill, *Narrative Unity*, 2:246–47; Susan Marie Praeder, "The Problem of First-Person Narration in Acts," *NovT* 29 (1987): 193–218.

19. Steven M. Sheeley, *Narrative Asides in Luke-Acts*, Ph.D. diss., Southern Baptist Theological Seminary, 1987. See also Sheeley, "Narrative Asides and Narrative Authority in Luke-Acts," *BTB* 18 (1988): 102–07.

20. Tannehill, *Narrative Unity*, 2:106. On "point of view," see Powell, *Narrative Criticism*, 23–25, 52–54.

21. The terminology derives from E. M. Forster, *Aspects of the Novel* (New York: Harcourt, Brace, Jovanovich, 1927), 67–78. See Powell, *Narrative Criticism*, 54–55.

22. Tannehill, *Narrative Unity*, 2: 24–25. Cf. 1: 253–74.

23. The connection between this period of instruction and the disciples' noticeable improvement has also been noted by redaction critic Richard Dillon in *From Eye Witnesses to Ministers of the Word: Tradition and Composition in Luke 24*, Anbib 82 (Rome: Biblical Institute, 1978).

24. See Gerard Genette, *Narrative Discourse: An Essay in Method* (Ithaca, NY: Cornell University Press, 1980); Powell, *Narrative Criticism*, 36–37.

25. Tannehill, *Narrative Unity*, 2:252–61.

26. Ibid., 2:201–03.

27. Ibid., 2: 74–76. See also Genette, *Narrative Discourse*, 113–60; Powell, *Narrative Criticism*, 39; Susan R. Suleimann, "Redundancy and the 'Readable' Text," *PT* (1980): 119–42.

28. Ibid., 2: 34, 47.

29. Joseph B. Tyson, *The Death of Jesus in Luke-Acts* (Columbia: University of South Carolina Press, 1986).

30. Charles B. Puskas, Jr., *The Conclusion of Luke-Acts: An*

Investigation of the Literary Function and Theological Significance of Acts 28:16–31, Ph.D. diss., St. Louis University, 1980.

31. Tyson, *Death of Jesus*, 43. Cf. David P. Moessner, "The Ironic Fulfillment of Israel's Glory," in *Luke-Acts and Jewish People*, 35–50.

32. Tannehill, *Narrative Unity*, 2: 348–57; idem, "Israel in Luke-Acts."

33. Ibid., 2: 352–53.

34. Luke T. Johnson, *The Literary Function of Possessions in Luke-Acts*, SBLDS 39 (Missoula, MT: Scholars Press, 1977).

35. Susan Marie Praeder, *The Narrative Voyage: An Analysis and Interpretation of Acts 27—28*, Ph.D. diss., Graduate Theological Union, 1980; idem, "Sea Voyages." Cf. Tannehill, *Narrative Unity*, 2: 330–43.

36. Murray Krieger, *A Window to Criticism: Shakespeare's Sonnets and Modern Poetics* (Princeton: Princeton University Press, 1964), 3. Cf. Powell, *Narrative Criticism*, 8.

For Further Reading

Achtemeier, Paul J. *The Quest for Unity in the New Testament Church*. Philadelphia: Fortress Press, 1987. Analyzes discrepancies between Acts 15 and Galatians 2 and concludes that Luke's account is theologically driven, if historically inaccurate. See above, 14, 90–91.

Barrett, C. K. *Luke the Historian in Recent Study*. London: Epworth Press, 1961. Briefly surveys a number of works dealing with Luke as a historian and discusses the problems in approaching his writings as history. See above, 83.

Bock, Darrell. *Proclamation From Prophecy and Pattern. Lucan Old Testament Christology*. JSNTSS 12. Great Britain: Sheffield Academic Press, 1987. Studies Luke's use of the Old Testament in light of his christological interests, emphasizing a sequential development of christology from the gospel to Acts. See above, 44–45.

Bovon, Francois. *Luke The Theologian*: *Thirty-Three Years of Research. (1950–1983)*. Allison Park, PA: Pickwick Publications, 1987. A detailed survey of Lukan scholarship, translated and updated from a French original in 1978.

Brawley, Robert L. *Luke-Acts and the Jews*: *Conflict, Apology, and Conciliation*. SBLMS 33. Atlanta: Scholars Press, 1987. Argues that Luke ties Gentile Christianity to Judaism and appeals to Jews to accept it as such. See above, 16, 69–70.

Brown, Schuyler. *Apostasy and Perseverance in the Theology of Luke*. AnBib 36. Rome: Biblical Institute, 1969. Studies Luke's concept of temptation and faith and argues that the evangelist stresses the faithfulness of Jesus' disciples so as to insure a reliable transmission of apostolic tradition. See above, 65.

Cadbury, Henry J. *The Book of Acts in History*. New York: Harper & Brothers, 1955. Provides context for understanding Acts through discussion of various cultural environments, including the ancient Near Eastern world in general and Greek, Roman, Jewish, and Christian environments in particular.

Cadbury, Henry J. *The Making of Luke-Acts*. London: SPCK, 1958. A classic study that treats Luke as an author in his own right and examines the literary process that resulted in his two works. See above, 5.

Carroll, John T. *Response to the End of History: Eschatology and Situation in Luke-Acts*. SBLDS 92. Atlanta, GA: Scholars Press, 1988. A study of Lukan eschatology which concludes that Luke thought the end was imminent and sought to summon believers to preparedness. See above, 59–60.

Cassidy, Richard J. *Society and Politics in the Acts of the Apostles*. Maryknoll, NY: Orbis Books, 1987. Refutes the notion that Luke attempts to foster an essential compatibility between church and state and argues that, instead, he prepares Christians for possible persecution. See above, 73–74.

Chance, J. Bradley. *Jerusalem, the Temple, and the New Age in Luke-Acts*. Macon, GA: Mercer University Press, 1988. Discusses the role that Luke believes Jerusalem and the temple are to play in the new age of salvation that has dawned. See above, 60.

Conzelmann, Hans. *The Theology of St. Luke*. 2nd ed. London: Faber and Faber, Ltd., 1960 (German original, 1957). Interprets Luke-Acts from the perspective of a three-stage model for salvation history developed in response to a delayed parousia. See above, 18–19, 58–59.

Dibelius, Martin. *Studies in the Acts of the Apostles*. New York: Charles Scribner's Sons, 1956. A collection of classic essays on various topics, including interpretations of the speeches and the travel narrative in Acts from the perspective of "style criticism." See above, 29–32.

Dupont, Jacques. *The Salvation of the Gentiles*. New York: Paulist Press, 1967; reprint 1979. A collection of essays by this French scholar on such themes as universalism, Pentecost, conversion, community of goods, and Luke's use of the Old Testament. See above, 67.

Dupont, Jacques. *The Sources of Acts*: *The Present Position*. London: Darton, Longman, and Todd, 1964. An historical survey of theories on Luke's sources for Acts which concludes that it is impossible to identify any of these with certainty. See above, 33.

Easton, B. S. *Early Christianity*: *The Purpose of Acts and Other Papers*. Greenwich, CT: Seabury Press, 1954. Contains an important essay, originally published in 1936, which argues that Acts presents Christianity as a legitimate religion under the leadership of a Christian Sanhedrin. See above, 15–16, 62.

Ellis, E. Earle. *Eschatology in Luke*. FB. Philadelphia: Fortress Press, 1972. Presents a two-stage model (present and future) for understanding Luke's concept of eschatology and salvation history. See above, 62.

Epp, Eldon Jay. *The Theological Tendency of Codex Bezae Cantabrigiensis in Acts*. Cambridge: Cambridge University Press, 1966. Demonstrates that an anti-Jewish bias underlies the variant readings in the Western text of Acts. See above, 22.

Esler, Philip. *Community and Gospel in Luke-Acts*. Cambridge: Cambridge University Press, 1987. Combines sociological research with redaction criticism to examine the role of Luke-Acts in providing social legitimation for Luke's community. See above, 17–18.

Fitzmyer, Joseph A. *Luke The Theologian. Aspects of His Teaching*. New York: Paulist Press, 1989. A collection of essays on a variety of themes, including authorship, discipleship, Satan and demons, and the Jewish people. See above, 34, 36.

Flender, Helmut. *St. Luke*: *Theologian of Redemptive History*. Philadelphia: Fortress Press, 1967 (German original, 1965). Offers an alternative to Conzelmann's view of salvation history and eschatology in Luke-Acts by proposing that Luke presents the exaltation of Jesus as the consummation of salvation in heaven. See above, 60–61.

Franklin, Eric. *Christ the Lord. A Study in the Purpose and Theol-

ogy of Luke-Acts. Philadelphia: Westminster Press, 1975. An overarching study of such matters as eschatology, christology, and ecclesiology that tries to situate Luke within the mainstream of Christianity. See above, 46–47.

Garrett, Susan R. *The Demise of the Devil. Magic and the Demonic in Luke's Writings*. Minneapolis: Fortress Press, 1989. Studies Luke-Acts against the background of contemporary ideas concerning magic and the supernatural, concluding that Luke presents Jesus' ministry as an overthrow of Satan. See above, 66.

Gärtner, Bertil. *The Areopagus Speech and Natural Revelation*. Lund: C. W. K. Gleerup, 1955. Interprets Acts 17:22–31 in a way that is basically compatible with Pauline theology. See above, 92, 99.

Gasque, W. Ward. *A History of the Interpretation of the Acts of the Apostles*. 2nd ed. Peabody, MA: Hendrickson, 1989. A detailed survey of literature through the 1960s, augmented by an article on recent scholarship published in 1988.

Goulder, M. D. *Type and History in Acts*. London: SPCK, 1964. Offers a complex scheme for understanding the structure of Acts based on cyclical patterns and the use of Old Testament typology. See above, 26–27.

Hemer, Colin J. *The Book of Acts in the Setting of Hellenistic History*. Tübingen: J. C. B. Mohr, 1989. Argues for the essential historicity of material in Acts, based on comparisons with Paul's letters and information from the Roman world. See above, 85–86.

Hengel, Martin. *Acts and the History of Earliest Christianity*. Philadelphia: Fortress Press, 1980. Argues that Acts can and should be used as a source for reconstructing early Christian history and then sketches the history that can be derived from Acts. See above, 86.

Jervell, Jacob. *Luke and the People of God*. Minneapolis: Augsburg, 1972. A collection of essays espousing the author's view that Luke writes for Jewish Christians, addressing their questions about relationships with other Jews and with Gentiles. See above, 70–72.

Jervell, Jacob. *The Unknown Paul: Essays on Luke-Acts and*

Early Christian History. Minneapolis: Augsburg, 1984. A collection of essays written from the same perspective as *Luke and the People of God* on such themes as historicity, Luke's portrait of Paul, the Holy Spirit, and women in Acts. See above, 54, 93–94.

Johnson, Luke T. *The Literary Function of Possessions in Luke-Acts*. SBLDS 39. Missoula, MT: Scholars Press, 1977. Suggests that Luke's emphasis on possessions has implications that go beyond the literal consideration of how to handle wealth. See above, 105.

Juel, Donald. *Luke-Acts: The Promise of History*. Atlanta: John Knox Press, 1983. A general introduction to Luke-Acts that, following Jervell, interprets the two-volume work within the framework of Jewish crisis literature.

Kee, Howard Clark. *Good News to the Ends of the Earth: The Theology of Acts*. Philadelphia: Trinity Press International, 1990. Considers five important themes in Acts: Jesus, the Holy Spirit, Christian community, Outreach, and Witness. (The book appeared too late to be included in the discussions on these matters in this volume.)

Kilgallen, John. *The Stephen Speech: A Literary and Redactional Study of Acts 7:2–53*. AnBib 67. Rome: Biblical Institute, 1975. A detailed analysis that interprets this speech as a thoroughly redacted Lukan construction.

Krodel, Gerhard. *Acts*. PC. Philadelphia: Fortress Press, 1981. A standard introduction to the book of Acts; including an especially good description of historical problems. See above, 46, 87–89.

Lüdemann, Gerd. *Early Christianity According to the Traditions in Acts*. Minneapolis: Fortress Press, 1989. Separates tradition from redaction in every pericope of Acts and discusses the historical value of what is deemed traditional. See above, 84–85.

Maddox, Robert L. *The Purpose of Luke-Acts*. SNTW. Edinburgh: T & T Clark, 1985 (original, 1982). Considers the various theories as to why Luke wrote his two works and decides the best explanation is that he wished to reassure Christians of the validity of their faith in response to Jewish criticisms. See above, 17–18.

Marshall, I. H. *Luke*: *Historian and Theologian*. Grand Rapids: Zondervan, 1970. Argues that an appreciation for Luke's interest in history is essential to a proper understanding of his theology, especially as regards the principal theme of salvation. See above, 48–50, 75.

Mattill, A. J. *Luke and the Last Things*: *A Perspective for the Understanding of Lukan Thought*. Dillsboro, NC: Western North Carolina Press, 1979. Argues that Luke expects the parousia to come soon and rallies Christians to accomplish the mission they have been given. See above, 59–60.

Minear, Paul. *To Heal and To Reveal*. *The Prophetic Vocation According to Luke*. New York: Seabury Press, 1976. Focuses on Luke's understanding of Jesus as a prophet and of the disciples as prophets like Jesus. See above, 48.

Navone, John. *Themes of St. Luke*. Rome: Gregorian University Press, 1970. A collection of studies on twenty important topics, such as Conversion, Jerusalem, Prophet, Salvation, and Witness.

Nuttall, Geoffrey F. *The Moment of Recognition*: *Luke as Story-Teller*. London: Athlone Press, 1978. A brief lecture that calls attention to Luke's skill at telling a story.

O'Neill, J. C. *The Theology of Acts In Its Historical Setting*. London: SPCK, 1961. Dates Acts in the second century and interprets its theology as an expression of "early catholicism" similar to that of Justin Martyr. See above, 16–17, 25–26.

O'Reilly, Leo. *Word and Sign in the Acts of the Apostles*. *A Study in Lucan Theology*. Rome: Editrice Pontificia Universita Gregoriana, 1987. Examines the twin themes of preaching and miracles in Acts and the relationship of both to the Holy Spirit. See above, 53–54.

O'Toole, Robert F. *Acts 26*: *The Christological Climax of Paul's Defense* (*Ac 22:1–26:32*). AnBib 78. Rome: Biblical Institute, 1978. Proposes that Luke's main interest in presenting Paul's defense speech before Agrippa is not so much to defend Paul himself as to defend the Christian belief in resurrection of the dead realized in Jesus. See above, 99.

O'Toole, Robert F. *The Unity of Luke's Theology*: *An Analysis of Luke-Acts*. GNS 9. Wilmington, DE: Michael Glazier, 1984.

An exposition of major themes in Luke's theology, emphasizing God's plan of salvation in Jesus and the anticipated response of Christians to this. See above, 6–7, 39–40.

Parsons, Mikeal. *The Departure of Jesus in Luke-Acts. The Ascension Narratives in Context.* JSNTSS 21. Great Britain: Sheffield Academic Press, 1987. Offers insight into Luke 24:50–53 and Acts 1:1–11 based on literary theories concerning beginnings and endings in literature. See above, 9.

Pereira, Francis. *Ephesus: Climax of Universalism in Luke-Acts. A Redaction-Critical Study of Paul's Ephesian Ministry (Acts 18:23—20:1).* Anand, India: Gujarat Sahitya Prakash, 1983. A detailed exegetical analysis of this section of Acts with emphasis on Luke's hope of salvation for all people.

Pervo, Richard I. *Luke's Story of Paul.* Minneapolis: Fortress Press, 1990. A popular reading of the story of Acts from the perspective of a first-time reader.

Pervo, Richard I. *Profit With Delight: The Literary Genre of the Acts of the Apostles.* Philadelphia: Fortress Press, 1987. Argues that Acts should be interpreted as an early Christian novel intended to edify its readers. See above 11–13.

Pilgrim, Walter E. *Good News to the Poor: Wealth and Poverty in Luke-Acts.* Minneapolis: Augsburg, 1981. Interprets the Lukan material dealing with possessions in terms of messages that the evangelist wants to send to both the rich and the poor. See above, 78.

Richard, Earl. *Acts 6:1—8:4. The Author's Method of Composition.* SBLDS 41. Missoula, MT: Scholars Press, 1978. A comprehensive treatment of the Stephen speech, including attention to its stylistic features and redactional function within Luke's second volume.

Richardson, Neil. *The Panorama of Luke.* London: Epworth Press, 1982. A general introduction to Luke's two works.

Sanders, Jack. *The Jews in Luke-Acts.* Philadelphia: Fortress Press, 1987. Offers exegetical commentary on key passages dealing with the Jews and concludes that Luke is anti-Semitic. See above, 69.

Seccombe, David. *Possessions and the Poor in Luke-Acts.* SNTSU. Linz, 1982. Suggests that Luke's treatment of this theme is an evangelistic address to persons whose devotion to wealth prevents them from accepting Christianity. See above, 17.

Stronstad, Roger. *The Charismatic Theology of St. Luke*. Peabody, MA: Hendrickson, 1984. A study of Luke's presentation of the Holy Spirit and its work in the church. See above, 51–52.

Tajra, Harry W. *The Trial of St. Paul*. WUNT 35. Tübingen: J. C. B. Mohr, 1989. An analysis of Paul's trials before government officials in Acts against the background of extra-biblical knowledge of Roman legal proceedings. See above, 86.

Talbert, Charles H. *Literary Patterns, Theological Themes and the Genre of Luke-Acts*. SBLMS 20. Missoula, MT: Scholars Press, 1974. An analysis of the formal patterns Luke uses in composing his two works and the implications these have for their interpretation. See above, 7–8, 14–15, 26.

Talbert, Charles H. *Luke and the Gnostics: An Examination of the Lucan Purpose*. Nashville: Abingdon, 1966. Argues that Luke wrote his two-volume work to serve as a defense against Gnosticism. See above, 10–11.

Tannehill, Robert C. *The Narrative Unity of Luke-Acts*. 2 vols. Philadelphia and Minneapolis: Fortress Press, 1986, 1989. A study of Luke-Acts that uses modern literary theory to interpret each pericope within the context of the story as a whole. See above, 8–9, 70, 100–105.

Tiede, David L. *Prophecy and History in Luke-Acts*. Philadelphia: Fortress Press, 1980. Interprets Luke-Acts as an attempt to deal with the identity crisis faced by Jewish-Christians following the destruction of Jerusalem. See above, 70.

Tyson, Joseph. *The Death of Jesus in Luke-Acts*. Columbia, SC: University of South Carolina Press, 1986. A literary study of the way Jesus' death is presented in these writings, with special emphasis on development and resolution of conflict. See above, 104.

Walaskay, Paul. *"And so we came to Rome." The Political Perspective of St. Luke*. SNTSMS 49. Cambridge: Cambridge University Press, 1983. Argues that Luke intended his work to serve as an apology to the church on behalf of the Roman empire, in the interests of improving church/state relations. See above, 73.

Wilcox, Max. *The Semitisms of Acts*. Oxford: Clarendon Press, 1965. Identifies Semitic elements in Lukan language and style and discusses the possibility that these might reflect the use of sources. See above, 28–29.

Wilson, Stephen G. *The Gentiles and the Gentile Mission in Luke-Acts*. SNTSMS 23. Cambridge: Cambridge University Press, 1973. An in-depth analysis of this theme which suggests that Luke's primary interest is to show the incursion of Gentiles has taken place according to the will of God. See above, 67–68.

Wilson, Stephen G. *Luke and the Law*. SNTSMS 50. Cambridge: Cambridge University Press, 1983. Argues that Luke conceives of the Jewish law as applicable only to Jewish people and hence as non-binding for Gentile Christians. See above, pp. 6–7.

Zehnle, R. F. *Peter's Pentecost Discourse: Tradition and Lukan Reinterpretation in Peter's Speeches of Acts 2 and 3*. SBLMS 15. Nashville: Abingdon Press, 1971. Examines the speeches in Acts 2 and 3 as redactional expressions of Lukan concerns.

Collections of Important Articles

Cassidy, Richard J. and Philip J. Sharper, eds. *Political Issues in Luke-Acts*. Maryknoll, NY: Orbis, 1983.

Interpretation, vol. 27, no. 2, April, 1973.

Interpretation, vol. 42, no. 2, April, 1988

Keck, Leander and J. Louis Martyn, eds. *Studies in Luke-Acts*. Philadelphia: Fortress Press, 1980 (original, 1966).

Kremer, Jacob, ed. *Les Actes des Apôtres: Traditions, rédaction, théologie*, BETL 48 (Gembloux, Belgium: Duculot, 1979). Several of the essays are in English.

Review and Expositor, vol. 87, no. 3, Summer, 1990.

Talbert, Charles, ed. *Luke-Acts: New Perspectives from the Society of Biblical Literature*. New York: Crossroad, 1984.

Talbert, Charles, ed. *Perspectives on Luke-Acts*. Danville, VA: Association of Baptist Professors of Religion, 1978.

Tyson, Joseph, ed. *Luke-Acts and the Jewish People. Eight Critical Perspectives*. Minneapolis: Augsburg, 1988.

Some Commentaries

Bruce, F. F. *The Acts of the Apostles. The Greek Text with Introduction and Commentary*. 3rd ed. Grand Rapids: Eerdmans, 1990.

Bruce, F. F. *The Book of the Acts*. NICNT. Rev. ed. Grand Rapids: Eerdmans, 1988.

Conzelmann, Hans. *Acts of the Apostles*. Herm. Philadelphia: Fortress Press, 1987 (German original, 1972).

Haenchen, Ernst. *The Acts of the Apostles. A Commentary*. 14th ed. Philadelphia: Westminster Press, 1971 (German original, 1965).

Kilgallen, John J. *A Brief Commentary on the Acts of the Apostles*. New York: Paulist Press, 1988.

Krodel, Gerhard A. *Acts*. ACNT. Minneapolis, Augsburg, 1986.

Marshall, I. H. *Acts*. TNTC. Leicester, England: Inter-Varsity Press, 1980.

Munck, Johannes. *The Acts of the Apostles*. AB. Garden City, NY: Doubleday & Co., 1967.

Neil, William. *The Acts of the Apostles*. NCB. Grand Rapids: Eerdmans, 1973.

Willimon, William H. *Acts*. IC. Atlanta: John Knox Press, 1988.

Bibliographies

Mattill, A. J. and Mattill, Mary Bedford. *A Classified Bibliography of Literature on the Acts of the Apostles* (Leiden: Brill, 1966).

Mills, Watson E. *A Bibliography on the Periodical Literature on the Acts of the Apostles, 1962–1984*, NovTSup 58 (Leiden: Brill, 1986).

Wagner, Günter. *An Exegetical Bibliography of the New Testament: Volume 2: Luke and Acts* (Macon, GA: Mercer University Press, 1985).